W9-BEH-103

DPH

Destined Publishing House
264 S La Cienega Blvd. #750
Beverly Hills, CA 90211

Copyright © 2009 by Maubrey Destined

All rights are reserved by Maubrey Destined, and content may not be reproduced, downloaded, disseminated, published, or transferred in any form or by any means whatsoever.

This is a true story, told to my best recollection. Certain names have been changed to protect the privacy and identities of characters.

To invest in the Maubrey Destined brand, or for more information about special discounts for bulk purchases, please contact Destined Publishing House Special Sales And Investments at
Investments@MaubreyDestined.com

i

CONTENTS

PRELUDE

Before one can compose the greatest, most motivational, and inspiring literary masterpiece of all time, one must live the greatest, most motivational and inspiring life. One must also read the greatest, most motivational and inspiring literary masterpiece of all time, from front to back, with an open, humble, and believing heart- The Holy Bible!
-Maubrey Destined

"You're going to shave your Mohawk before going to court tomorrow, right?" I recall my older brother and mom asking me.

"No." I replied confidently, "I'm going to keep it."

Immediately, a very worried and concerned look appeared on both of their faces. You would think that a 21 year old man facing 60 years in prison would shave his Mohawk before the first day of his trial. But not me.

My mom and brother proceeded to try to convince me that I should shave my Mohawk before going to trial. They even called my father in New Jersey and asked him to talk to me. Still, I was not willing to shave my Mohawk.

There was a moment that night that I briefly considered removing my Mohawk, but then, as I looked myself in the mirror, alone in my bathroom, I changed my mind. I was so sure and confident that I would walk into and out of the flames of the trial victoriously, that I knew in my heart that there was nothing that could change the course of what God had promised me. Not even a Mohawk.

My mind, as in the past, was set! The next morning, on Valentine's Day, February 14, 2005, was my moment of truth!

I woke up early, showered, dressed up neatly, with my collared shirt and tie, said a prayer with my mom and brother, and drove them to the Bloomington courthouse. It was a cloudy day with lightly drizzling rain coming from the heavens. We parked directly in front of the courthouse. Together as a family, we walked up the courthouse stairs, into the building, and through the metal detectors.

As I led my mother and brother up the stairs to my public defender's office, my mind was as clear as the view of a serene lake on a cool autumn morning. I knocked, then gently turned the door knob and opened the door. We were greeted by the receptionist.

"Hi," I said humbly, "I'm here for my trial today. Can we go to Mr. Scott's Office?"

My public defender of the past two years was Wyatt Scott. That is the moment it happened! That's when the Lord and Savior, Jesus Christ's magnificent wonders, like the fulfillment of glorious revelation, began to unfold! That's when the goodness of Heaven began to shake! I get instant chills throughout my entire body, as I write! The receptionist looked absolutely puzzled.

"That's odd... I don't have you on his schedule today."

Now, I was puzzled! I turned my head to my mom and brother. Their faces were puzzled too! The receptionist was puzzled. I was puzzled. My mom was puzzled. My brother was puzzled. Everyone was puzzled!

Exactly what was unfolding before our very eyes? The receptionist took a second and third look at my defender's scheduled appointments for the day.

"No...No, I don't have you scheduled for the day."

"Are you sure?" I asked perplexed.

I restated my full name.

"I'm sure." she replied "Let me go to the back, and get Mr. Scott from his office."

While we waited, I thought, as had happened many times in the past two years, that the trial date was once again, continued to a future date. My family and I waited patiently.

"What are you doing here?!" my public defender said as he walked towards us.

"I'm here for my trial." I said.

And with the same irritated, annoyed, and extremely busy look that he seemed to always have on his face, he shook his head from left to right.

"You didn't get the letter in the mail?"

"What letter?" I replied.

He seemed to have become even more irritated. He let out a laugh of annoyance, and shook his head once again.

"Follow me to my office!" he instructed us.

My brother, my mom, and I all looked at one another even more confused than ever. I didn't know what to think. When we got to his office, he shuffled through his desk and handed me some paperwork.

"Maubrey," he said, as he began to read the paperwork, "Your case has been dropped!"

My heart... It jumped! My chest... It warmed! Endorphins rushed throughout my entire body! I lifted my eyes from the paperwork and looked at my lawyer in the eyes. I turned to my mom and brother, who had flown over 1000 kilometers from New Jersey to a little town in Bloomington, Indiana to support me for my trial.

Their faces seemed to be in a sudden state of shock and surprise. Just like that; it happened so fast! The entire moment seemed just too surreal. It was as if all time was moving in slow motion…as if I had been in a movie for the past two years unknowingly, and that hidden cameras were going to come out of nowhere.

My brother and mom's eyes widened and retracted quickly. I could tell that they were thinking exactly what I was thinking. I could almost hear the sweet sounding heavenly angels singing in my head, and trumpets playing in the background.

I had passed the test of God! His face was shining brightly upon me! After almost two and a half years of immovable believing, after I had put every cell of faith into the Lord Jesus, after I had stood strong in what Christ was whispering into my heart, after so many opportunities to give up, give in, and concede to the suggestions and beliefs of my friends, family, and the world, the Lord said, "My son, now I know that you are a true believer in Me!"

God had softened the heart of the judge. God had softened the hearts of the prosecutors. And God had even softened the heart of my public defender, Wyatt Scott.

I am absolutely positive that the words to the prosecution and judge that came out of Mr. Scott's mouth over the course of the previous two years could have been completely different, if he was not pushed to fight for me.

I do recall one specific afternoon, just shortly before that day, as I sat in his office, he was advising me as usual, to take a probation plea. I continued to hold my ground.

And then he did something out of the ordinary. He left his office and brought in a woman that I had never seen before. He told me to explain once again to the woman and him, why I thought that I did not deserve to go to jail or get probation.

I was not prepared to give a speech, and I had no idea who this new woman was, but I started to speak. A few sentences into my testimony, I had felt something spiritual come into me that I had never felt before.

That afternoon in that office with my defender and the woman, my words seemed to suddenly flow seamlessly. I poured my heart out about how drastically the experience of getting arrested had completely reshaped and redirected the course of my life – how I was a new man. I spoke of how I had learned my lesson. I spoke of how I would never sell drugs again.

Although they knew and disapproved of me selling the legal herbals, I made them understand that through my various businesses, I was making a valiant effort to avoid ever selling illegal drugs again.

I let them know how much optimism and enthusiasm that I had for my future as a result of what I had learned from the trying experience that I was living through, day in and day out.

The room stood frozen, with all attention focused on me and the words that were coming from my tongue. My eyes watered as the emotion behind my words overwhelmed me. I spoke until I could not speak any more. I purged my soul with all that I had. The Lord was surely speaking through me.

When I finished speaking, they excused me, and I never saw that woman again. Now that I look back, I beg to ponder, whether that mysterious woman was a prosecutor or the district attorney, whether she wanted to hear for herself, and see with her own eyes, what man of such faith and confidence in the Lord would adamantly turn down a treasure chest of mere probation, in confident and unwavering expectancy of a sea of riches of complete freedom.

Perhaps, she had to see for herself, whether I was pure, whether I was a renewed and changed man. For now, I do not know the answer. What I do know is that the Lord Jesus Christ saved my life from the moment that I was arrested. He rained favor on me even from the beginning, when, out of many choices, He appointed to me the county's chief public defender, with the most influence, credentials, and knowledge, Wyatt Scott.

With my mom and brother to my side, I remember reading the paperwork that stated the reason for my case being dismissed.

It read: "...The State of Indiana has dismissed the case against Maubrey Okoe-Quansah for the pursuit of justice."

That phrase always seems to amaze me each time I think of it.

"For the pursuit of Justice..."

Amazing! If the definition of justice is: the quality of being just; righteousness, equitableness, or moral rightness, then the state of Indiana had made a sound decision in their pursuits!

I wasn't quite there yet, but after that two year journey, I was more righteous. I was more just. I was more moral.

I thanked Wyatt for all that he had done for me over the course of the past two years. We shook hands, and he gave me some encouraging words and advised me to continue to stay out of trouble.

I really appreciated all that he had done for me. My family and I said our final "Thank yous" and "Goodbyes", then left Wyatt's office and exited the courthouse.

When we entered my car, the rejoicing and celebration began! Everything still felt so surreal. The feeling was indescribable! Through the lightly drizzling rain, there was much hugs, smiles, kisses, music and praise on the ride back to my home.

It had to have been one of the happiest days of my life. I had witnessed and experienced a true life miracle! A miracle on Valentine's Day!

And ever since finding out that my case had been dismissed on February 14, 2005, every year, Valentine's Day has had an extra special meaning to me.

It was truly the day that Jesus showed His love for His son!

When we arrived at my town home, the celebration magnified! Music was in the air! There was dancing! There was jumping, rejoicing, and many more hugs! We popped bottles of champagne! I remember dancing on top of my bar countertop.

By then, the word of my great deliverance had spread rapidly. Cell phones began to ring continuously. Calls were coming in from my friends and family from all around the world!

We shared the celebration with my aunts and uncles from London. We shared the celebration with my family in Africa. The great news spread to New York and New Jersey. The news had spread to all my close friends on campus.

Everyone was so happy, and relieved especially, that I was now officially a free man.

But, on the contrary. I was a free man all along, from the moment I trusted in Christ!

We celebrated the victory with a big feast that my mom had prepared that afternoon, and then at night, my brother and I went over to my best friends' apartment to be with the amazing friends who had stuck by me the entire time.

Gavin, Landon, and Stella embraced and congratulated me as I walked through their door with my older brother. Still young and foolish, we chose to celebrate with drinks and marijuana. I felt that I needed the high after what I had been through for the past two years.

The next day, my family was gone. On the plane back to their normal lives they went, away from "The Maubrey Destined Movie" that I called reality.

Now, it was back to business again. I had been given a new lease on life! I spent the next few months left in the school year, training vigorously for the NFL supplemental combine. I increased my intensity, became even more focused, and eliminated distractions. It was now time to prepare for my destiny!

The Maubrey Destined *Effect*

The Journey to The Kingdom of Heaven

May this book move, inspire, and motivate you to higher levels that you have never even fathomed. May this book reveal the secrets of unlocking all of your hidden gifts and finally obtaining absolute and total happiness!

Chapter 1

Soon, I was squatting more than ten repetitions of over 460 pounds, and I was sprinting at accelerated speeds. I was bigger, faster, and stronger. I had never felt and looked so good in my entire life. I had traveled to a higher dimension. My friends and complete strangers began to take more notice of my transformation.

I even recall, for months, suddenly getting full page, sometimes multiple page, sexually explicit love letters on the windshields and side windows of two of my cars, as well as at my door step, well past midnight.

The secret admirer would awake me from a deep sleep with the sound of my doorbell ringing. When I would open the door, I would see another love letter on the floor.

It seems that one of my affluent neighbors had taken notice of me during my many shirtless, sweaty runs through the complex and into the neighborhood. Week after week, I would get random notes. I was flattered, however I was also concerned. I would show my friends the letters and always asked for their opinions about how to handle it.

Of course, you could guess what my hormone driven, sexually charged friends would say, but I had changed so much since freshman year, that I wasn't like that anymore. Had I gotten these sexual letters during my first year in Indiana University, or even the previous year, when I wasn't focusing on getting into the NFL, I probably would have even left replies with my phone number on my cars.

Then finally, after months of getting these sexually explicit, absolutely graphic letters, I received the final letter that the supposed girl who was writing me all these letters was actually a man!

Yes...I said a man! He wanted me to meet him at a park, just footsteps away from the border of our apartment complex. I was completely caught by surprise. I had to laugh. But this was my life. This was "The Maubrey Destined Movie" that I was living in.

When I told my friends the finale of all the sexually explicit letters, they all burst out laughing. And they laughed for days. It was quite comical. But it would give me early insight to what kind of unwanted attention that I would be receiving, and how to gracefully handle fame, lust and love from strangers in the future.

Another afternoon, I had invited my friends over to The Boulders to relax in our newly completed pool and spa. Two of my best friends, Gavin and Landon were relaxing in the Jacuzzi, when an attractive woman in her late thirties joined us.

I recall noticing her husband (or ex husband) and children in the background near the pool. The woman had her toddler in her hand, who for some reason, took an immediate liking to me. The baby girl could not take her big blue, adorable eyes of off me for some reason. That may have been the most adorable baby I had ever seen.

The mother, who began to flirt with me even as her husband (or ex husband) waded in the pool, allowed me to hold her toddler. To make a long story short, later that evening, my friends and I went out to a nightclub. At about 3 A.M. in the morning, when we were exiting the nightclub, out of nowhere comes walking the woman from the spa! I couldn't believe my eyes. I had never seen her in the past four years that I was in Bloomington, but all of a sudden, there she was, walking towards my friends and me, with a cowboy hat on her head, a blouse, tight blue jeans, and cowboy boots on her feet.

You could tell that she was a bit intoxicated. She left the man that she was with, walked with us for miles, in and out of side streets of Bloomington. She made subtle sexual remarks to me throughout the walk.

When we all finally arrived at my best friends' apartment, that's when the woman started complimenting, flattering, and flirting with me excessively. I tried my best to resist, but my friends wanted everything that woman had to offer.

However, like a cougar in an African jungle, she had her mind and eyes fixed solely on me.

Before I knew it, she was sitting with us all, completely nude on a couch in my friends' computer lounge room. Still, I tried to resist, but she seduced me with her amazing body. I took a condom out of my wallet and started having sex with her on the couch as my two friends hovered around both sides of her like sharks attempting to get her to orally please them.

It was quite comical to me. Less than a minute after having sex with this woman who I had just met about 12 hours before, I had to stop. I just felt so wrong. I couldn't get her toddler's face out of my mind. Not to mention the fact that I may have been committing adultery, even though I hardly had any conception of the word at the time.

It had been one of my fantasies to have sex with a married woman, and also for my friends and me to have sex with one woman, but it just didn't feel right.

After stopping, I told her that I'd be right back and left her in the room with my friends to continue having sex with her. I remember avoiding her by hiding in the apartment for the rest of the night.

Early the next morning, I quietly snuck out of the apartment and drove off to The Boulders before anyone was awake. What a night! Yet another addition to my wild sex life.

Oddly, there were too many similar sex stories like that. Over the course of that year, I had had sex with ex girlfriends, Italian girls from New York, nursing students outside at night, by my apartment complex's hot tub, random girls that I had just met in front of nightclubs, and so on. I was a sexually charged machine. And the interesting thing is that, during my fourth year in Bloomington, I spent more time rejecting, and turning down much more sexual offers from women, than I did, in having sex with them.

By my fourth year on campus, I had had sex with well over 20 women. I lost count after a few years. And if it weren't for my selectivity in women, and self-control, I surely would have had sex with literally hundreds of beautiful women. I am just thankful that I never contracted a single disease along the course of my promiscuity, and that I was at least wise enough to always use protection, with the exception of less than a handful of times with Stella.

Finally, after many months of intensive training with my trainer and great new friend Max, in the spring of 2005, it was time to travel to Azusa, California for the NFL supplemental combine.

I had never worked so hard for something in my life! I had come such a long way from the man that Max saw in the nightclub, to a man more focused and determined than ever. I had given it everything that I had during those training sessions. I had weathered the storm. I left no stone unturned. I was ready to go to California for the first time in my life!

I had dreamed of going to California ever since I was five years old. It is amazing how the Lord causes past dreams to come to fruition during the pursuit of another. The week before my flight to California, Max treated me to a surprise dinner. I remember after our last intense practice together, him telling me, "I've got a surprise for you... Make sure you don't eat." I smiled. He really believed in me and the work that we had accomplished together. He gave me much encouragement. He let me know that I had his full support, when I traveled to California alone.

When I arrived at LAX airport in California, I hardly had enough money to afford a hotel. As usual, I had all of my money invested. Fortunately, I met a man at the airport who was there for the NFL combine as well. He kindly offered to share a hotel room with me, free of charge. I was truly blessed for that connection. I was prepared to sleep outside the tryout facility overnight, if I had to.

That night in the hotel, I received calls from friends and family wishing me good luck for the following morning. I was truly grateful. When I arrived on the field the following morning, there were hundreds of athletes, just like me, who were there to try to get into the NFL.

What would be a very long day began. We were tested on our speed, strength, quickness, and vertical leap. I had one of the top vertical leaps, 38" inches of that year. However, I was only able to bench press the standard 225 pounds a total of 8 times. My quickness was descent, however, my speed was the lowest. I ran a 40 yard dash on grass at a disappointing 5.2 seconds.

After seeing my 5.2 seconds time, my heart dropped. I could not believe that I had run that slowly. With a few more routines to complete, I knew that there was no way that I would qualify for the next round in Indianapolis, Indiana.

There are high schoolers, and even heavier weighing people who could run faster than that. I wanted to give up and not participate in the other tests, but I did not. I pressed forward, and completed the long, tiring day.

One truly inspirational image that I will never forget about that day, was seeing a middle aged, short, balding man with glasses, trying out with us men, who were mostly in our early twenties. The man had extremely limited quickness or speed, and had not an ounce of muscle on his body. And it wasn't as if anyone could try out for the NFL combine. Before getting invited, you had to pay hundreds of dollars and get approved. I recall everyone laughing at the top of their lungs, every time it was his turn. Once, he even fell flat on his face while running, and everyone laughed even louder.

I however, did not laugh. I just recall standing there looking at him, with a bewildered look on my face, wondering why he was wasting his precious time and money trying out.

I later realized that the Lord had purposely placed the man there as a true inspiration for me. He wanted to show me that no matter how much you fail in life, as long as you believe wholeheartedly in Him, and you never give up, then you will achieve the dreams that He has placed in your heart.

I wonder where that man is now. I am sure that he is living his dreams, whatever they are.

I was disappointed in my performance that day, but I flew back home with my head held up. When I arrived back to Bloomington, I had a lot of critical decisions to make. Was I going to give up on my dreams? Was I going to move back home to New Jersey with my parents? Was I going to stay in Bloomington for a fifth year, and train for next year's NFL combine while continuing to sell the herbal drugs? All of my best friends were graduating in a matter of weeks. What direction was I going to now follow on my long journey?

After a few weeks of careful thinking, I decided to press forward on what had been on my mind the entire year, and virtually all my life. I was going to move to the place of my dreams. I was going to move to the "city of angels", Los Angeles, California! I was going to boldly go there on pure faith, then figure a way out to get on one of the three NFL teams in California.

I had no idea how I was going to make it on a team. I just knew that I had the drive, the will, and persistence.

I knew absolutely no one in California, however, by then, with all that I had overcome in the past few years, I was surely convinced that I could do anything if I put my trust in the Lord!

And going to Azusa, California for the NFL tryouts, although it was quite a distance from Los Angeles, gave me the extra boost of motivation to follow through with my lifelong dreams!

But before I would go there, I was going to fly to Tallahassee, Florida to regroup and spend the summer with my brother and his roommate, who was a close Ghanaian family friend of a similar age. We called him our cousin. My brother had wanted me to visit him in Florida for so many years. Now was the time.

One by one, after graduation, my friends were leaving campus, most, never to return again. I had witnessed this familiar scene many times – the sudden emptiness of campus after a long school year. This time, I would not be around for the warm, summer, Bloomington nights. I felt so sad that I was leaving. It was comparable to the time I had to leave camp in the sixth grade. I could almost cry. I could not believe that this adventurous chapter in my life was coming to an end.

I started selling and giving away all my possessions. I could only take two or three suitcases on the plane to Florida. A few weeks had gone by. I had sold and given away everything but my black BMW that I had recently bought. It was the hardest thing for me to decide to sell my BMW. Not for materialistic reasons, but because of the fact that selling it would symbolize complete closure. Selling it would mean that I had nothing left in Bloomington to keep me there.

Finally, I sold my car! It was my time to move forward once again.

Wow…!

My four years in my own paradise bubble that I had created was over. I had sold around $100,000 dollars of drugs and herbals to thousands of Indiana University students. I had made tons of lifetime friends. I had had sex with dozens of beautiful women. I had learned many valuable life lessons. I had overcome many obstacles and adversaries. I had conquered many fears and witnessed many miracles. My faith in Christ had strengthened. My wisdom and knowledge had expanded.

I came to Indiana University a 17 year old boy. I was leaving a young man. It felt like it was only yesterday, that I, a wide-eyed, naive boy from Irvington, New Jersey, stepped out of the airport shuttle bus and arrived in front of the Indiana University Memorial Union Hotel. It felt like only yesterday, that I lost my virginity in my freshman dormitory room. It felt like only yesterday, that I was handcuffed, arrested, and was facing 60 years in prison for drug dealing. It felt like just yesterday, that I was checking into a homeless shelter.

Oh, how fast the universe seems to have moved, as you reflect on the wonderful paradise that you experienced. From my birth in Germany to being taken to Ghana, Africa. From Ghana to the basement in Brooklyn, New York. From the basement to the second floor, from the second floor to Madison Avenue Elementary School in Irvington, New Jersey, from Madison Avenue Elementary School to Union Avenue Artistically Gifted Magnet School, from Union Avenue Artistically Gifted Magnet School to Thurgood Marshall Artistically Gifted Magnet School, from Thurgood Marshall Artistically Gifted Magnet School back to the new Union Avenue Artistically Gifted Magnet School, my journey continued. From the new Union Avenue Artistically Gifted Magnet School to Myrtle Avenue Middle School, from Myrtle Avenue Middle School to Frank H. Morrell High School, from Frank H. Morrell High School to Eigenmenn Dormitory in Indiana University, from Eigenmenn Dormitory to Foster-Harper Dormitory, still I journeyed. From Foster-Harper Dormitory to the University Commons Apartment Complex, from the University Commons Apartment Complex to Monroe County Jail and back, from the University Commons Apartment Complex to living with friends, from living with friends and briefly living on my own, to living at Woodlawn Apartments. From Woodlawn Apartments to a homeless shelter, from a homeless shelter to president's quarters, from president's quarters to The Boulders!

Now, the spirit of Christ was leading me to Tallahassee, Florida! What discoveries lay before me, I had not a clue. I shipped tens of thousands of dollars worth of the herbals overnight, to my brother and cousin's place in Florida, warning them not to open the package until I arrived.

I said my final goodbyes to all my closest friends who were still in Bloomington. Words can't express how sad I was during the final weeks, knowing that I wouldn't be able to see my best friends on a constant basis again.

They really made me who I had become. I would miss them dearly. But it was time to move onward!

Landon, my right hand man, who had given me a ride to the homeless shelter just a year before, was now giving me a ride to the airport shuttle bus early that spring morning.

I felt that same exact feeling in the air, during that short car ride to the airport shuttle bus as I did, when he drove me to the homeless shelter. This was it! I was actually going to go through with it! Landon must have wondered how in the world I was going to survive. But he had seen me do it before. He knew that I would prosper once more, somehow, someway!

Before I exited his car, I thanked him for everything that he had ever done for me over the course of the past four years. We shook hands, hugged and said our final goodbye.

A few hours later, I was cruising on a plane, at about 600 miles per hour, more than 30,000 feet in the sky!

Chapter 2

Florida.

I finally arrived at Tallahassee Airport that evening. This was my first time returning to Florida since visiting in high school. I was a long way from Bloomington. I had entered a new matrix – a new dimension!

My brother and cousin, Anthony, were there to pick me up from the airport. There were smiles and laughs at first sight of one another. You could immediately tell that something exciting and mischievous was going to arise during my stay.

This was my first time meeting Anthony. We only spoke a few times on the phone, telling jokes and sharing brief anecdotes. It was like looking at my brother's twin. I could not help but laugh as I approached them at the airport. They were the same height. They had the same dark skin tone. They had the same white teeth. They had the same build. They even spoke alike.

"This is going to be interesting." I thought to myself.

We hugged and continued to laugh and smile. Anthony and my brother, who was now going by the name Samuel, helped put my luggage in the trunk of the car, then ushered me to their one story, three bedroom house near Florida State University campus.

I had gone from one party school, Indiana University, to another, Florida State University. When I arrived at the house, the first thing I noticed was the large pool table in the middle of the living room. Then there was Shadow, the adorable black kitten that was but a few months old.

They showed me what was to be my room for the summer. The room was fairly cluttered and used for storage, but it had a full size bed for me to sleep in. I was just fine with that.

That first night, as we traded stories, I'll never forget the anxious and disoriented feeling that I had in my head. I had never felt that way in my life before. It was culture shock! My spirit came out of my body, soared into outer space, looked at the planet, and then pinpointed exactly where on the earth my body was, realizing how far I was on the globe from my bubble paradise of Bloomington, Indiana.

Suddenly, I was missing Bloomington more than I had ever imagined! My mind greatly expanded that very night. It was as if I had traveled to another dimension after getting on that plane! I realized then, that I had been in a heavenly matrix, a matrix nonetheless, for the past four years of my life. It took me about a week to fully adjust and become comfortable with my new environment.

Tallahassee was quite a unique and interesting town. It is the capital city of Florida. There are three large colleges and universities, Florida State University, Tallahassee Community College, and Florida Agricultural and Mechanical University, all within a 12 mile radius, with a total of over 70,000 mostly sexually charged students.

Florida State University had a top ranked football team. It seemed that football was always the topic of everyone's conversation.

The weather was absolutely gorgeous, with just a few minutes of sun-showers on most days. There was much humidity and heat in the air, and lovely palm trees everywhere. And it seemed as if everyone was looking for a big opportunity. With these types of statistics, my mind immediately began to work in overdrive! Something outrageous was bound to happen during my stay.

After I got settled in the house, I opened the fresh package of herbal powder, pills, and capsules that I had shipped from Bloomington. I now had tens of thousands of dollars of legal drugs! Now, I just had to sell it.

Some days went by without me selling a single pill. I wasn't sure who to trust, and I remained patient, studying and learning the different ways that things operated in Tallahassee.

But then, when the time was right, and I had learned the environment, I introduce herbal ecstasy to the Florida market in a major way!

I had found my zone! I was starting to create my own paradise again. I felt like I had teleported from one heaven to a better heaven. I reinvented myself. I started shaving my head for a clean bald look.

Under the beautiful Florida weather, my daily attire was tank tops, shorts, slippers, diamond bezel watches, and over $1,000 combined dollars worth of Chanel, Bvlgari, or Gucci high-end, luxury, designer sunglasses that a non-paying, former customer in Bloomington gave me as collateral for the herbals.

That summer, for me, was pure euphoria with my brother and cousin. I did nothing but wake up, eat, workout, go to pool parties during the days, meet new people, network, sell herbal drugs, make an abundance of money, and then end the day by going to parties and nightclubs with my brother and cousin.

In the beginning, college girls would literally circle me like sharks in nightclubs. I'm not sure if it was my confidence, my looks, my constant bright smile, my amazingly toned body that I had worked so hard for, the expensive sunglasses that I wore, the diamond bezel watches, or a combination of all of the above.

I laugh and shake my head at the fact that I say "diamond bezel watches" remembering that, on some nights, I used to wear two watches at the same time. You could easily say that my style and fashion taste was unique, even at the age of 21 years old. Anyone who noticed me could immediately tell that I surely was not from Tallahassee, or Florida, or from the planet, for that matter.

My brother and cousin were hilarious whenever we all went out. They would always hype me up to women they met, in order to get them to the house to have sex with them. They would tell them that I was going to the NFL, and sometimes, that I was already in the NFL. Other times, they would tell them that I was rich.

For me, it was always good to be surrounded by beautiful women, however, continuing my goal that I had set out to achieve, just before leaving Bloomington, I was no longer focused on having sex with as many random women as possible. My focus was solely on making as much money as humanly possible, and training to get to the NFL. I even contemplated staying in Florida, and trying out for one of the three NFL teams there – the Jacksonville Jaguars, the Tampa Bay Buccaneers, or the Miami Dolphins.

Chapter 3

Fortunately, the Lord brought Taylor into my life just at the right time. Less than a few weeks of living in Tallahassee with Samuel and Anthony, one night, before it was time to go to a nightclub, they told me that they were going to invite the perfect girl for me to go out with us. I was automatically excited! No one, especially family, who knew me, and my taste in women more than anyone else, had ever said that they had the perfect girl for me! They knew that I was extremely selective, and that I loved tall, thin, exotic, unique looking, beautiful women.

"She's in my architecture class." Anthony said, "You'll love her!"

I thought to myself, "Smart, creatively artistic, and beautiful?"

I became more excited! I remember the first time that I ever laid eyes on Taylor Wilson. We had arrived in front of her house later that night in Anthony's SUV. Anthony and my brother were sitting on the front seat. I was conveniently sitting in the back seat. I could see, barely, in the dark, a silhouette of a woman walking from the house towards the car. I had on brown leather sandals, cargo shorts, and a bright, yellow Abercrombie & Fitch, sleeveless fitted shirt. When Taylor walked into the SUV, it was as if I was looking at an angel! My senses were immediately captivated and awaken by the smell of her sweet aroma. I was thrown off guard by her long flowing hair. Her eyes were an endless ocean. Weighing about 125 pounds, and standing about 5' feet 9" inches tall, with a size C-cup bust, her body was absolutely perfect! Her physique was slender and toned. Her skin was glowing like a bronze statue. She radiated pheromones. My hormones burst with explosion inside my body.

"How in the world," I thought to myself, "Am I so fortunate, that my cousin was friends and classmates with such an amazingly beautiful woman?"

You could not tell my excitement by the nonchalant look that I had on my face. Taylor smiled at me and said "hello" to my brother and cousin. There was definitely an intense chemistry at first site. Anthony introduced us, and then we were on our way to the nightclub.

We had a few conversations during the ride, rotating back and forth with the boys in the front seat. Before arriving at the nightclub, I already had a plan of action. It had to be perfect if I was going to win her heart.

I had so many tricks up my sleeve that I had used in the past, in Indiana University to seduce women. This time, I was going to go with my instincts. I was going to completely ignore her from the moment we exited the car, and have a great time dancing with, and kissing other women in the nightclub.

For the next couple of hours, during that evening at the nightclub, that's exactly what I did. I barely saw her, with the exception of a few times that I saw her glancing into my direction as I sexually danced with and kissed two other college women on a stage. We smiled at one another. I could tell that my mischievous plan was starting to work. The chemistry was definitely growing, as the hours went by.

After the nightclub, in the parking lot, we seemed to have been magnetically drawn to one another. My heart raced as we subtly flirted with one another. I had a few drinks in my system. She seemed even more heavenly. I can't forget us facing one another and holding hands, and me leaning forward to kiss her for the first time, when she leaned backwards. My heart sank. She shook her head, as we stared deeply into one another's eyes. We both exchanged smiles. She had a boyfriend, who was away for the summer! He was also friends with Anthony, and was in her and Anthony's architecture class.

That meant nothing to me! I had found my princess, when I was least searching. I was prepared to be patient. After exchanging numbers and dropping Taylor home that night, I could not get her off my mind. We spoke on the phone and got together a few times for the following days.

Then finally, one night, just before she was about to leave our house, I finally got my first kiss! I lick my lips now, as I am transported back in time to the exact moment, alone with Taylor, in that small, dark foyer of the house. It was like kissing a heavenly angel. How soft, sweet, and moist, her lips were as they pressed against mine. How she melted in my arms, as I ran my fingers through her silky, long hair with one hand, and caressed her neck with the other. My heart pounded. My chest warmed. I was deeply in love!

Sometimes, I wondered how I was so fortunate to meet a girl, to meet a woman, to meet a princess like Taylor.

We were so different, yet exactly alike. From different worlds we came from, yet together at last, at that moment in time. Nothing in the world mattered, but the deep, sudden, love and attraction that we had for one another! We hesitated to leave one another's arms.

Our love blossomed from that night onward. We sent constant love text messages back and forth to each other. We spoke on the phone every chance that we had. We got together at every opportunity.

Then finally, after weeks of using my charm, and whispering sweet nothings into her ear, we made love to sweet music, under the midnight stars, in the tiny, cluttered, storage bedroom that I slept in. It felt as if we became one, that night. Our love was consummated!

Meanwhile, the longer that I stayed in that house, the more I began to realize that my older brother and cousin had made the house into a bachelor pad oasis. It seemed as if every time I turned around, or came out of my bedroom, there was a different college girl in the house.

Sometimes, I would come out of my room with no shirt on, and wearing only shorts. The entire room would shift to me. It always put a smile on my face. These Floridian, southern women were a different breed, different from what I had been used to in Bloomington.

My brother and cousin always tried to set me up with the random women, but I always declined. I already had my princess.

Tallahassee was certainly an interesting town. Living there, this time around, was like nothing I had ever experienced. There were so many amazing nightclubs, the police officers were so laid back and down to earth. It seemed that half of the officers had just graduated from one of the three colleges. One would immediately notice how lenient and friendly they were. I recall us getting pulled over while intoxicated or under the influence of the herbal ecstasy at least three times that month, and managing to talk our way out of them all.

Then there was the incident, in the VIP section of a club, when I sold a student a few herbal pills for him and the girls that he was with. I was sitting there, dressed sharply, with my dark designer Bvlgari sunglasses on, diamond bezel watch around my wrist, head clean shaved bald, enjoying the music and the scene, with a big smile on my face. I had taken an herbal pill a few hours before. I was feeling happier than usual. The guy gravitated towards me and started a conversion with me. Within minutes, I sold him a handful of pills that I always kept on me.

I didn't notice him for the remainder of the night, until after the night club was closing, and when there were hundreds of drunken college students congregating outside the club.

"I want my money back!" I suddenly heard from the guy who was behind me.

By that time, I was floating on cloud nine. I wasn't worried. I had seen this many times before. I assured him not to worry, that the effects would kick in soon. I even lifted up my sunglasses, showing him how dilated my eyes were from taking the same pills. He had been drinking too, after taking the pill that I sold to him. He said that his female friends that he had bought some for also did not feel a thing.

"It had been less than an hour since I sold it to them." I thought to myself. "They need to be patient."

The drunk and frustrated student was not willing to be calmed down. All he knew was that he wanted his money back. With a carefree smile on my face, I continued to exit the nightclub into the sea of drunken students as he continued behind me.

The next thing I know, I felt a fist hit the right side of my face! If you would, just imagine me with my black designer sunglasses on, wearing a tank top, showing off my muscular arms, standing about 6' foot tall and weighing close to 185 pounds at the time, when a shorter, but bigger and stockier guy just punches me from behind. It was a comical sight. I hardly felt a thing. I was still actually cheerful as I picked up my sunglasses that his punch had knocked to the floor.

My brother and cousin, who saw me get punched from a distance, unfortunately did not share the same empathy as I did. Before I knew it, commotion broke loose in the crowded parking lot. Both my brother and cousin had managed to punch the guy in his face.

Meanwhile, still in mental bliss, I was attempting to mediate. Eventually, both parties were separated. The guy and his girls walked away to their parked vehicle.

But the story did not end there. For some strange reason, I decided to go to the guy and girls, as they entered their SUV to assure them not to worry, that the effect of the pills would kick in soon.

I always stood 100% behind the products that I was selling. I even offered to give them back double and triple their money back if they didn't feel the effects later. I did not want a single unhappy customer in Florida. But the guy was still steamed, and still wanted his money back. The girls on the other hand, were much friendlier, and were willing to give me the benefit of the doubt. I continued to assure them as they entered the SUV.

"You can get in and talk." one of the beautiful girls said to me.

For some strange reason again, I didn't think twice about getting in the SUV with them. Perhaps, I was that confident in the product. We proceeded to drive away. The guy calmed down a bit, but still wanted his money back. The girls attempted to mediate as I continued to assure them.

All of a sudden, I had realized that we had driven to a secluded area near the far rear of the nightclub. The guy's temper suddenly began to increase again, substantially.

"I want my money back now!" he began to shout again.

All of a sudden, I saw two cars full of drunk, belligerent college men, abruptly pull up to where we were parked. It was the friends of the guy and the girls that I was in the car with! I realized that as I was attempting to calm the guy down during the short ride, one of the girls or the guy must have called or discreetly texted the gang of college kids.

The guy, now brave, since he had help, stormed out of the SUV demanding that I come out of the car, and give him back his money. I immediately panicked! I felt like I was suddenly in a scene of a very bad movie. I was being ambushed! I had never been in this dangerous situation before. I had no idea what to do, as I nervously sat alone in the back seat of the SUV.

Two of the girls, I believe, were still in the front seat. Everything was happening so fast! His belligerent friends circled the SUV. For the first time in my dealing days, my life and well-being was surely in danger, and there was no one around to help. I tried reaching for my cell phone to call my brother or 911.

"You better not touch that phone!" the guy profaned loudly.

I was trapped with no way out! It was a frightening scene. There was a lot of shouting and yelling from the guy and his gang. Still, I refused to give him back his money.

Suddenly, I saw them attempting to open the car door that I was cornered next to. I quickly locked the door. They became more angered and enraged.

Next, they tried to drag me out of the SUV by my legs. I used all my strength and kicked them away. The girls, fortunately, favored me, and attempted to protect me from being attacked by the gang.

"Please, just give him back his money!" one girl pleaded with me.

Suddenly, I saw one of the guys breaking the bottom of a beer bottle. Now, I had definitely seen this scene in a few violent movies. It just felt surreal! Now, I was experiencing it in real life, in real time. A girl screamed. My heart raced! No amount of money was worth being cut or stabbed with a broken glass bottle! I had to think very fast! I was running out of time.

"Ok..!!" I finally yelled.

I reached into my pocket and gave him back his money.

"Get out of the car!" he yelled, after taking the money.

Was the angered mob still going to attack me? There had to be at least ten of them. I remember sizing all of them up. I knew that I could fight them each individually, or even as a whole. But with the broken glass bottles and other weapons that they had, there was no way that I would stand a chance. I braced myself for the worst. By the grace of the Lord, my eternal Protector and Savior, the moment I exited the SUV, they all ran to their cars, and quickly sped away.

Chapter 4

I was left alone that night in the back lot, with my heart still pounding from the close call. I counted my blessings. I knew that Christ had definitely covered me with His shield of protection! Only the Lord could get one out of such inevitable harm.

I immediately called my brother and told him to come and pick me up. I told him and my cousin all about what I had just been through. They thought that I was insane when they saw me getting into the SUV with the guy that they had just punched. They figured that since there were girls, I must have had everything under control. It must have been about 4 A.M. in the morning, still dark outside.

My brother and cousin arrived and took me to another nightclub that stayed opened much later. Then suddenly, after being in the nightclub for about 30 minutes, I got a call. I smiled and shook my head, as I looked at the number on the caller ID on my cell phone.

Lo and behold, it was the guy and the girls from the previous club, who I was almost attacked by. I knew exactly why they were calling. When I answered the phone, he gave me a sincere apology for reacting the way he did. The pills that he and the girls bought from me had activated, sending them to a state of pure euphoria.

"It's ok. I understand," I said, "That's what I had been trying to tell you all along."

He wanted to meet with me the next day to return the money he had forced me to give him. I remember driving to a newspaper box, near a fast food restaurant to pick up the money a few nights later. He must have had second thoughts about meeting me in person, after thinking about what he had put me through that night. I could not blame him. So in the end, I got my payment back and at the same time, witnessed a man of honor. I found it very rare for a man that I didn't know to return money after all that had happened that night.

Tallahassee…!

What an experience those nights out were. I cannot even begin to fully describe the outrageousness that resulted each time we went out. It surely lived up to its reputation as a party town.

Meanwhile, my sales were steadily high, until one hot afternoon, when I met a guy named Christian through another contact. Against my better judgment, I agreed to meet him and the girl that he was with in a backyard of what seemed to be a vacant house.

It was a completely open space. As I surveyed my environment, I nervously imagined being watched by the DEA or Tallahassee Police Department from any of the houses that surrounded us. And I could never forget the girl he came with. She was a petit young girl, probably in college, who had big dark sunglasses on, and didn't say a word the entire time.

The contact who was introducing us was there as well. However, I barely knew him either. I remember trying to make the introduction go as fast as possible that afternoon. We small talked for a bit, and then I gave him two or three few samples. Christian told me that he and his incognito girl would try the pills out immediately and get back to me later that night. If they liked it, they would repeatedly buy a few hundred at a time, possibly thousands at a time.

And then, just like that, we parted ways, got into our separate cars, and drove away. I honestly thought that, like some of my past new clients, he only said that he would buy in bulk in order to get free samples. I thought I would never see him again. But I didn't worry. It would be a small loss if that happened.

How wrong, was I. Later that evening, I received a call from Christian raving about how much he loved the pills and how out of this world the effects were. We laughed together. I knew we were in business! He wanted to buy over 100 pills immediately.

Of course, I became excited inside. However, my nerves were raised. I had seen this movie before. Although the pills were legal, there was no way that police in Florida would know that. If I were being set up, then I would surely be arrested and taken to jail until all was discovered. I was not in Bloomington anymore!

I went with my instincts. I agreed to meet him. Thinking back, I realize how the fear of being harmed or killed rarely crossed my mind. I always seemed to be more concerned with whether my buyers were working for the police, than whether I would be killed. I recall shaking Christian's hand and telling him to be careful, as I exited his old, run-down car.

The big deal was complete! I had made about $1,000 dollars. I remember patiently waiting for the next couple of hours in the house to see if the DEA would come kicking in the door. It never happened. Less than three days later, Christian returned to my neighborhood.

This time, not with the same old run-down car, but with the latest, brand new leather interior car. His clothes were brand new and his hair was neatly shaved. Almost overnight, Christian had transformed into a new, different person. That is the instant effect of drug dealing that lures so many people. He had sold out of the original few hundred pills that I sold to him. I smiled. I had finally found someone as ambitious and risk taker as me!

For the next straight weeks of my stay in Florida, Christian kept returning, and returning, and returning to buy more and more of my herbals. I could barely keep up with the demand.
Sometimes, he would buy a few hundred pills, travel across the border to Georgia, and sell out, then come back after midnight and buy a few hundred more.

Christian and I were making thousands upon thousands of dollars together! It was a euphoric time of my life! I had never made so much money, that quickly in my life! I spent more time depositing cash into the ATM than I ever had. Each time Christian came, we both had big smiles on our faces. We were both helping each other make a lot of money.

"They call it the 'blue kahuna!'" Christian joked about the pills.

In a short time, Christian and I quickly developed a strong bond. We both seemed to understand that making money wasn't only about spending it recklessly, but about making a change for our lives, giving away some to others, and accomplishing our goals and dreams.

Soon, it wasn't just a business relationship. We became friends. I remember taking rides with him in his brand new car a few times. We talked about everyday life. We talked about family. We talked about relationships and women. We talked about our long term goals, and just gave each other positive motivation. We talked about how we wanted to quit dealing soon. I told him about my professional football dreams. He told me about how he was starting a truck distribution company. We talked about his home town of Atlanta, Georgia. I had never been there. He even invited me, should I ever decide to visit. He even went out of his way to drive me a few hours away, just to take me to a discount outlet flea market, to buy inexpensive luggage for my approaching relocation to Los Angeles.

All this kindness from a person that I had only met but a few weeks ago. Christian sure was a good man. I could tell that he had a pure heart. Perhaps, that is the reason why the Lord paired us together, despite the sins that we were committing.

Christian had no idea that the pills were legal though. I was glad to know that if he were ever caught, that he would have to be set free eventually. With the help of Christian, and the dozens of customers that I had quickly made during my short time in Tallahassee, I had completely sold out!

I had made well over $10,000 dollars in a matter of weeks! And I still had customers calling me constantly for more. But my time in Tallahassee was up! I came, I saw, and I conquered! Like a shrewd businessman, I came into a new land, saw an opportunity in a huge market, and capitalized greatly by introducing a new and different product.

To me, this was pure business. It was a happy, but sad time for me. I was moving to the place of my dreams, but leaving the girl of my dreams. During that month together, Taylor and I had become so hopelessly in love with one another. She was my darling princess. And I was her prince.

If she only knew that her boyfriend was a major dealer. I doubt that she would have judged me though. During my final two weeks in Tallahassee, we spent much time, and many late nights together. We would miss each other dearly. I remember cuddling together on the sofa talking about whether or not to remain a couple when I moved to California.

She tried to convince me to stay in Florida and tryout for the NFL teams there. But I couldn't. California was calling me. I had to go. Still, she was ready and willing to stay as a couple when I moved, however I had to seriously think about it. I had never been in a long distance relationship in my life. I didn't know if I could trust myself to stay faithful when I moved to Los Angeles, over 2000 miles away. I did not want to break her heart. I loved her too much.

In the end, I agreed to give it a try. I could not have chosen a farther place to be from her. Florida was all the way in the southeast tip of the United States, and California was in the farthest, most western part of the country. This was going to be a true test of love for me!

In the beginning, I told you that my life was truly complex, consisting of infinite surprises at every turn, consisting of many dynamic layers. The plot thickens! It thickens indeed!

Throughout my cathartic journey with you, from my birth until now, from time to time, I have googled names, places, and memories that had been brought back to life. Travel through time, from the year 2005 in Florida, into the future with me again.

It is present day. The month is February. The year is 2010. Just a few moments ago, after telling the story of my herbal sales for so long, I decided to google the name of my former supplier. And what I discovered immediately after, was nothing short of shocking!

My former supplier had been arrested! Not back in 2005, not a few years ago, not even a year ago, but only a few months ago from this day. My former supplier had been arrested on federal charges for mail fraud, misbranding a drug, introducing goods into domestic commerce by means of false statement, and criminal forfeiture.

In plain terms, my former supplier is accused of selling a chemical found in cough medicine, called DXM, as an "herbal" alternative. I do remember now, that some of my past clients did say that they thought the effects felt like DXM.

The indictment also states that my former supplier mailed several packages of the drug to several places into a handful of states including California and Indiana! My former supplier is now facing up to 20 years in prison, paying hundreds of thousands of dollars, and seizure of their valuable possessions!

It took me some time for the shock to settle. Shock and surprise doesn't seem to stay with me for much long anymore. If anything, it is expected in my everyday life. That is simply the dimension that I've been living in for quite a while now.

When the initial shock subsided, I honestly considered destroying all these writings, that for the past 8 months, I have given my heart and soul to. But then, I was reminded by the Lord, deep in my spirit, that I had already been warned and groomed for this pivotal point, that the devil would make his final attempt to cause me to abort, and prevent me from completing these amazing works. I had surely foreseen this stumbling block. I must press forward, sacrificing myself, for the sake of truth! I am a new man, saved and forgiven! No more is there fear of the enemy! No more is there fear of man!

The spirit of Christ has made a permanent home inside my body! I know now that goodness and mercy follows me all the days of my life. And what the devil means for evil shall always be turned to good! I must set a faithful example to those who look up to, and are inspired by me! How can I write what I have written, and live how I have lived, and still have fear!? I cannot! I will not!

Now, well over five years later, a revelation has been made. You see, that's the thing with lies… They can go on almost forever, then suddenly return deep into the future, when you least expect it. The truth, no matter how long it is buried deep in the dark, always comes to the light! The truth is the only answer!

All that time, I thought that I was lying to my customers, but now, it seems that I, in fact, may have been lied to the entire time. I think of how many times that I ingested and sold the pills, believing that they were natural herbals. But, I am certainly not one to pass judgment. Perhaps, they really are herbals, and the lie comes from another source. Either way, I will forgive, just as Christ has forgiven me time after time again for my many sins and trespasses. Without my past, my wisdom would be altered.

Now, hold my hand, and journey with me again back through time to a quiet and virtually empty airport in Tallahassee, Florida. My brother and Taylor had just given me a ride to the airport. I had recorded my princess, Taylor, saying goodbye to me on my cell phone's camcorder, I gave her a long, passionate kiss and hug before walking inside the airport terminal with my brother, who was helping carry my luggage. This was it! My emotions ran wild as I looked at my brother. What a wild summer! A summer to remember! It is true when they say that time flies when you're having fun.

It seemed like just yesterday, that I had arrived from Bloomington, Indiana, and saw Anthony and Samuel with the big smiles on their faces and shiny black bald heads. Now I was going to the land of the unknown, with no planned place to live, absolutely no friends or family, and no idea what to expect.

My luggage was now checked in. My brother and I gave one another a big hug, and then I boldly strode forward into my future, never looking back!

I will greatly cherish, and always remember the many new friends and amazing times that I experienced in Tallahassee. The good was great, and even the bad was good in that wild college town.

I recalled the petty arguments that young drug dealers around the corner from the house, who were in their late teens, all the way down to 9 years old, had with one another. They would get angry whenever the other would sell to a customer on their turf. I remember looking out the window thinking, "If they only knew and understood that all they had to do was network, and that they didn't have to stay on the block under the hot sun all day."

In the airport, I also thought about the simple pleasures that I loved and enjoyed, like driving out to eat at the Florida State University campus food courts. My usual specialty was piles of hot Belgian waffles on a plate, covered with strawberry sauce, whip cream, and drizzled with maple syrup. I always had a big appetite.

Then, there were the times that my brother, Anthony, Taylor and I would come home from a party or nightclub late at night, then entertain and amuse ourselves by calling late night infomercials, and give them fake credit card numbers in funny voices. We would laugh and laugh all night!

Overall, I loved just about everything about Tallahassee. I almost ended up staying, but I knew that I had to follow my dreams. One can easily get trapped in that enchanting matrix of a town for years, without even noticing time flying by.

Chapter 5

Later that evening, finally my plane landed at LAX – Los Angeles International Airport! I was here! I could feel it in the air, that I had entered a very different world. All alone, it was time to do what I did best – Believe!

With thousands of dollars in my pocket, but with no place to stay, I told the airport shuttle driver to take me to a nearby hotel, I quickly realized that all the luxury hotels that I would have preferred to stay in, were all hundreds of dollars per night. I had no intention of wasting money, no matter how much I had.

Finally, after driving around Downtown LA for some time, late that night, I saw a motel with a sign that advertised "Only $39 per night." That was it for me.

I thought to myself, "If I'm not going to stay in a five star hotel, then I might as well stay in the cheapest motel possible."

I thanked and tipped the shuttle driver, then checked into my first living quarters in Los Angeles. It wasn't bad at all. My room was clean, the bed was comfortable, and there was a television.

There was nothing that could match that feeling that I had in my body that night. I was actually in Los Angeles! The dream that I had, ever since I was five years old in that tiny, one bedroom, basement apartment in Brooklyn, after coming from Africa – now at only 21 years old, I was actually now living it!

It felt like I had fallen out of the sky, got up, dusted myself off, and landed in a lucid dream! The smell, the sounds, the lights, the beautiful palm trees, the feel, the atmosphere... I loved and embraced it all that night in my small motel room.

That night, I spoke to my friends and family in New Jersey, Indiana, and Florida until I fell asleep.

There is nothing like waking up in the morning in a new state for the first time! After I had showered and dressed up, in my usual, tank top, shorts, and slippers, I took a morning walk in search for food. I quickly realized that I would certainly need a car soon.

For over a week, I called that humble motel home. I had my routine. I would wake up, do a few hundred pushups, shower, go out to get food, then spend the majority of the day on the phone and in the Los Angeles Library computer lab trying to find an apartment to live in. I do not miss those long days.

Finding a good apartment in LA wasn't as easy as I imagined, even though I had thousands of dollars in cash. It also did not help that I had been evicted so many times in Indiana, and that my credit was not good. After more than a week of living in that motel, I started to get a bit frustrated with my environment. I needed to relocate to maintain my harmony.

Fortunately, my brother knew a female friend from college, who lived in LA. She was happy to drive me around LA and help me find a hotel. Finally, after looking at a few low grade hotels with her, I finally decided to check into a four star Marriott hotel. Since my cousin worked for the hotel chain at the time, I was able to get a discount for about a week.

About ten stories above ground, I enjoyed the beautiful views overlooking a rooftop pool and lounge area. I could see my bright future far into the horizon. Day after day, still, I searched for apartments, walked for hours under the hot sun from apartment complex to another, getting my applications rejected again and again because of my credit.

A bit discouraged, I pressed forward each day. Before I knew it, my cousin's employee discounts had run out, and still, I had no apartment. It was time to move again. Then I moved to another low grade hotel near downtown, LA. I was sensing a familiar theme that I had experienced all my life. Except, it was at a much accelerated pace in LA.

Now, instead of relocating every year, I was now relocating after less than a few weeks. Next, I went to another Marriott hotel, just a few minutes away from the airport. Fortunately again, one of my good friends knew a girl that worked at the desk. I was able to get a slight discount for a few days.

Then again, her employee discounts ran out as well. Now, I was paying close to $200 dollars per night for the hotel room, not to mention food costs, transportation fees, and other expenses. My time and money was depleting each passing day. I had to think and move faster. I was not in Bloomington, Indiana anymore! The friendly hotel staff used to joke whenever they saw me come out of the elevator into the lobby in the morning.

"Do you live here now?" or "You're still here?" they would joke.

It always made me smile. But at the same time, I knew that my money wouldn't last forever. At nights, I would go downstairs to the bars for some drinks in the lobby, or get a taxi to the nightclubs in Hollywood. When I first started going to nightclubs in Los Angeles, I wasn't too impressed. Possibly, because I had built up so much anticipation from the glamorous images I had seen all my life, or perhaps because, at first I did not know which nightclubs were the best to go.

Nevertheless, I continued to explore. Soon, I started networking at the nightclubs, selling the pills, and exchanging numbers for the future. I invited a few random people up to my hotel room to buy pills. At night, it was back to the nightclubs.

I can't forget the first time I saw a celebrity in Hollywood. I was standing in line to enter an A-list celebrity nightclub, when, no other than my childhood role model, Hulk Hogan, ushered his way in, less than a few feet away from me. How fitting that the first celebrity I would see in my childhood dreamland, would be one of my childhood role models. I loved him since I was about five years old, and now I was standing less than five feet away from him. He was bigger than life! For the first time, I knew what it felt like to be star-struck. That surely ended up being an amazing and memorable night.

The strangest thing happened to me another night out. I recall going out to a club at Universal Studios in Hollywood after taking one of my herbal pills. As the taxi cab raced up the spiraling hill to the location of the club, I recall the effects starting to kick in. It was then, in the back seat of the taxi cab, that I had a sudden enlightenment that the world, since the beginning of time, has been going in a perpetual cycle, a wonderful circle of never ending repetition, with no ending, a machine that never stops running.

It blew my mind, as my spirit seemed to soar out of my body, deep into outer space, as I looked at exactly what pinpoint of the world that my body was. I was actually in Hollywood! It is true what they say about one's mindset, the first time going to Hollywood. Here I was, more than a month there, and still, I had not yet wrapped my mind around the reality. As if the night wasn't strange enough, my young, now 22 year old, inexperienced to the world mind was blown away soon after.

I had just turned 22 that week. I was in a massive crowded nightclub in Universal Studios, with my designer $400 dollar, dark Bvlgari sunglasses on that night, when out of nowhere, a guy, around the same age as me, dressed nicely with the exact same sunglasses on, came up to converse with me. I had never met the guy before, we instantly had a connection, and within minutes of talking, he started telling me his life story. It was totally surreal. I listened in that loud crowded club, as he told me that he had been recently arrested for selling hundreds of ecstasy pills, and that he was out on parole.

He talked and talked. My mind was blown! I did not share my story with him, of what I had been through with my case for the past few years. I simply stood there listening in awe.

For the first time, I realized that there were other people going through almost the exact same situations and circumstances as me. It was just absolutely enlightening to hear him talk. He had no idea who he was telling his story to. His story hit so close to home, that I began to get suspicious.

Was he an undercover or informant strategically placed in my path to get close to me? Was I being watched from Indiana, to Florida, to Los Angeles, by federal drug enforcement agencies? That thought had always been in the back of my mind.

At that time, he was holding both my and his identical $400 dollar sunglasses in his hand, as we laughed and complemented one another on our tastes in sunglasses. When he handed my shades back to me, I suddenly became untrusting. I thought for some reason, that his shades were fakes, and that he had switched our identical shades while I wasn't paying attention.

At that time, the effects of the herbals had peaked. I spent much time accusing him that his shades were fakes and that he was trying to scam me. He was so insulted, especially after forming such a fast bond with me, and sharing his personal story with me. I refused to give him both sunglasses until I was finished examining the sunglasses. Looking back, it was obvious that both of our sunglasses were 100% authentic.

Finally, after minutes of examining, I finally gave him the sunglasses that I felt were his. I'll never forget the humiliated and hurt look that I saw on that good man's face. I had severely insulted a potential lifetime friend. What he did after, just boggled my mind. He didn't throw a punch at me. He didn't spit on my face. He didn't even curse at, or insult me. The guy's feelings were so hurt, that he took his $400 dollar shades that I had given back to him, looked me in the eye, and without hesitation, broke them in half!

"You think I would cheat you!?" he exclaimed.

Writing now, more than four years later, I almost feel tears coming from my eyes. I had become so untrusting, paranoid, and materialistic, that I had absolutely disgraced a good and honest man. I was so ashamed. I have done many wrongs in my life, however, that accusation, in my mind, is one wrong that I truly regret, and am ashamed of the most.

I never saw the guy again after that night. I learned a very, very valuable lesson that night!

Chapter 6

The following mornings, after going out, would be back to business as usual – Find an apartment! After about a month of spending hundreds of dollars per day to live in a hotel, I had to make a change. I had to find somewhere else to stay that was less costly.

Next, I found an Extended Stay hotel in the area, where customers would get a reduced price by paying for a week or more in advance. It cost me about half the price of living in the previous hotel. It was no apartment, but at least I was saving my funds.

Now, in about a month and a half in Los Angeles, I had already lived in a motel and four hotels! I was racing against time to find a one bedroom apartment. No landlord would allow me to move in without a co-signer. No one in LA, nor my parents would co-sign to lease an apartment for me. I was running out of options. The possibility of having to leave Los Angeles crossed my mind many times. I stayed persistent however.

Then one evening, after calling a taxi cab driver to pick me up from the hotel that I was staying in to take me to a nightclub, the driver started a conversation with me. I was open and friendly as usual. He asked me what I had moved to LA for, and I began to tell him that I wanted to play professional football. I told him that I was looking for a trainer to get me faster. He immediately had a trainer in mind for me to contact.

"Peyton Moore." the driver said the trainer's name was.

The taxi driver told of how his son, who was around my age, and on the University of Utah football team, trains with him and has one of the fastest 40 yard dash times in the country. I became excited! He had my attention. That was exactly what I wanted to hear. That was exactly the type of trainer that I needed! Before exiting the cab, I exchanged numbers with the driver, and also took the number for Peyton Moore.

Days later, I met with the trainer, Peyton, just a few blocks from my hotel. He picked me up in his gold Lexus coupe. I told Peyton, as I had told my former trainer and good friend in Bloomington, exactly what my goals were of breaking the world record, becoming the fastest man alive, and becoming the greatest athlete of all time! After spending a few hours with him, I was convinced by his knowledge and shared vision with me.

I was inspired! I felt that we were on the same page. I felt that he not only believed, but had the wisdom and experience to get me to my goals and beyond. Before he dropped me off, back to the hotel, however impossible it may have seemed to be to find a home, I assured him that I would hire him as a trainer immediately after I found an apartment.

My fortune continued. Soon after, came the day that I was first discovered by a photographer! I had set up an appointment to look at a beautiful, resort styled apartment complex, one hot Los Angeles afternoon. Still with no car, and not wanting to waste money on a taxi, I decided to walk the 15 minutes that the directions said it would take. Not knowing the neighborhood, I suddenly realized that I was lost. Under the intense heat, I wandered farther and farther away from the apartment complex.

I was becoming hungry and dehydrated. Fatigue was setting in. Hours had gone by of what was supposed to be a brisk 15 minute walk from the hotel to the apartment complex. As the sun beamed on my face, I began to think that it was a sign from God, that I was not supposed to be in Los Angeles. Nevertheless, forward I pressed.

Finally, after hours of walking under the blazing sun, and numerous phone correspondences with the apartment management team, I had finally arrived at the entrance of the apartment complex.

The place was heavenly! Like I had entered a resort in Cancun, Mexico. I recall speaking to my best friend, Gavin on the phone as I entered the compounds. Something was quite unusual. There was over a dozen people grazing the compounds, just outside of the management office. I immediately noticed that they all had one thing in common, as I continued to walk forward. They were all amazingly beautiful people!

"Oh...wow...! I think I've hit the apartment jackpot!" I joked with Gavin on the phone. "You have to see this," I exclaimed with excitement, "Everyone who lives here looks like a model!"

Gavin became excited, just as I told him that I had to get off the phone. I had to be focused if I had just discovered a secret paradise! With my casual pants, and my usual sandals and revealing tank top on, I smiled as I entered the building.

"Hi, are you here for the audition?" I recall a friendly lady behind the desk as me.

"Oh...no," I said confused, "I'm Maubrey. I'm here for my appointment to see an apartment."

"Oh, ok." she replied with a smile.

"You can have a seat there with the rest of the models. Someone will be with you soon."

After sitting and talking with some models and a photographer's assistant for some time, I learned that there was a model open-call for a hair product photo shoot. The assistant asked me if I was next. I turned my head and looked around.

"Oh no, I'm not a model." I continued, "I'm just here to look at an apartment."

He seemed to have had a surprised look on his face. He continued to have a conversation with me, encouraging me to model. He gave me the name and number of the photographer, who was conducting the interview in the conference room.

"You should definitely talk to him when he is finished seeing all the models."

I was in awe, and caught by surprise. I certainly did not wake up that morning with any motivation or desire of becoming a model. And, although friends and complete strangers had suggested it in Indiana and Florida, I certainly did not come to Los Angeles to pursue modeling.

But the Lord had another idea, a greater vision for me! The child that He had brought into this world to create beautiful art, but abandoned it as a rebellious adolescent, was going to be brought back into the world of art! This time, through a different window. Christ has mysterious ways of bringing us back into our destiny.

At that very moment, a new fire had been rebirthed! I would pursue my athletic dreams, and call the photographer, Zachary Anderson, who happened to live in that apartment complex, as soon as I found an apartment.

All of a sudden, it seemed that everything expected and unexpected was falling into perfect divine order. Unfortunately, I was not able to rent the apartment there, again, because of my lack of, and poor credit. My soon to be trainer, Peyton, who suggested the complex to me, even attempted unsuccessfully, to try to help me get the apartment there. With flowing waterfalls streaming down tall boulders, palm trees, a glistening pool and three hot tubs, I promised myself that I would live in that apartment one day. Christ had shown me a taste of paradise again, and I would be back!

Finally, just as my situation seemed hopeless, I found a nice one bedroom apartment for rent in Koreatown, just minutes from the Downtown area of Los Angeles. I decided just to be honest and said to the apartment manager, "My credit is not too good. I can't get a co-signer, but I can deposit more than a few months of the $1,100 per month rent. Can you help?"

By the grace of God, the friendly Korean manager was willing to ask the owners of the small, four story boutique building near the corner of Virgil Avenue and the busy Wilshire Avenue, to allow me to move in.

About a day later, I received the miraculous news! I was elated! After over a month of sweat, uncertainty, and searching, not only was I able to get an apartment in a good location, but once again, I was able to get it at a discounted price.

In addition, the beautiful building and my cozy apartment had recently been completely remodeled. The Lord, once again, had put me through a trying test, and rewarded me for my unmoving persistence, determination, and belief in Him. I had truly been blessed yet again!

Chapter 7

Now that I was finally settled, I was ready to chase my dreams, full speed ahead! Between modeling, football practice, my online businesses, stocks, and dealing herbs, I was going to be a very busy man. I immediately called a handful of my past clients that I had sold pills to, in Indiana, Florida, and California.

Within a matter of days, I was shipping thousands of pills nationally. Just like that, I had emerged into a full blown drug lord, shipping packages of what I knew to be legal herbal pills throughout the country! This was what I wanted all along. I craved to be the biggest dealer in the country. I craved to be the biggest dealer in the world!

Soon, clients were flying across the country, to Los Angeles, to buy from me. I felt like I was in a surreal movie. I was gaining more and more customers each time I went out to nightclubs. Los Angeles had never seen the pills that I had introduced to the scene. Money was flowing abundantly. My bills were always paid on time.

With the combination of my looks, personality, and especially the fact that I was a dealer, I was being invited to all the best A-list celebrity nightclubs in LA. I didn't have a car yet, so I always went out in a chauffeured, black town car limousine. I was living the life of a celebrity. It was almost unbelievable. In my mind, I had stumbled onto a hidden gold mine. I was utilizing my brain to take advantage of every opportunity and idea that the Lord sent my way.

I had no fear of getting arrested, since I knew that the pills that I was selling were herbals. Then, there was still the danger of being killed or robbed. Nevertheless, I was fearless. I treated every customer as if they were my family or best friend. I could sense and avoid anyone with negative energy. It was a gift that the Lord had given to me, to keep negativity away for so long.

Weekly, I would manage calls from customers in Florida, Indiana, California and a few other locations, who wanted more and more pills. I could barely keep up with the demand.

Then there was my online business. I started selling e-books online about how to start internet businesses, investing ideas, and also my workout routine that I did to achieve my toned body. It was truly an exciting time in my life. Money seemed to be coming from every direction. But I was far from complacent. The more money that came in, the more time I spent in my tiny, one bedroom, cozy basement apartment, thinking and brainstorming ways of multiplying it.

Plus, I had not forgotten why I had come to Los Angeles in the first place. I was there for football. Days after I had moved into my new apartment, I called the trainer, Peyton Moore. I think back now. If he only knew that his soon to be client was a national drug baron…

I always made sure to keep my drug life far away from my normal life. The journey of training again began. Now, I was paying about $250 dollars per session, for Peyton to train me. I wanted to get into the NFL badly! I was willing to do whatever it took. I was willing to pay whatever I had to pay to work with the best. I put my trust in Christ that I was making all the best decisions to fulfill my destiny.

I'll never forget the day that I first saw the iconic "Hollywood" sign. I was in the car with Peyton, returning from a training session. Peyton was counseling me as we navigated through traffic that sunny afternoon. The road we were on was on a hill. As he spoke, suddenly I looked in the distance. And there it was! Far ahead, the image that I had seen and dreamed of since I was about five years old in my parents' small, one bedroom basement apartment in Brooklyn. It was quite ironic. Here I was, more than fifteen years later, living in a small one bedroom basement apartment on the exact opposite end of the country, now marveling at that sign in person. My heart skipped a beat! I gasped, interrupting Peyton from talking.

"What's up?" he asked.

"It's the Hollywood sign!" I exclaimed as I pointed to the distance.

He laughed and shook his head. I had been in Los Angeles for months now, and hadn't seen it yet. To some, it is just a sign, but to me, it symbolized that dreams, even after more than 15 long years, do come true, if you are persistent in your believing in the Almighty Jesus! The iconic sign seemed to have shinned under the sun's rays as I marveled at it.

Around the same time that I called my trainer, Peyton, I also called Zachary, the photographer who was willing to take my pictures for free. We set a date, and in late 2005, my journey in creating art through modeling began!

All it took was one person to believe in me enough to give their valuable time to me, and I seized the opportunity! Now, what friends and strangers had suggested I do, had become a reality.

I remember packing a bag of some of my clothes, and Zachary picking me up to drive me around to shoot at different locations. After getting the pictures from Zachary, my confidence in myself and self perception had never been so positive. I knew that it was only the beginning. I can never thank Zachary and the man who introduced me to him enough for being the first to believe!

After weeks of intensive training and learning from Peyton, running up steep sand dunes, climbing mountain cliffs, and running multiple full speed sprints, it was now time to take a step of faith and walk on to the arena professional football team practice.

I didn't have a car yet, so for weeks, I woke up at the crack of dawn, and took a few busses to get to practice. The trip was more than two hours each way, however, it did not bother me. I was on a mission! I was always one of the first athletes there, and always one of the last to leave.

For weeks, I gave 100% of all that I had in me. I felt that I was making progress every day. At 22 years old, I was the youngest player on the field. I was practicing with former college All-American players and former NFL players. I listened as much as possible, and tried to soak up every advice that I received. Everyone seemed to be very helpful to me. I could visualize being on the team for the upcoming season.

Day after day, I would come to practice hopeful and energetic. At night, I would train with Peyton. This was my new routine – Go to practice, come home, eat, sleep, and then train with Peyton in the evening. I would eat upon my return, and then fall into a deep sleep.

At about 6' feet tall now, and 180 pounds, and virtually no body fat, my body was growing. It was climbing to its peak.

Finally, after about a month of tryouts, and handfuls of players gone, it was time for the management to choose the team roster. Unfortunately, after all that determination and commitment, I did not make the team. I was just not fast or quick enough. I was always just a step behind. My four years away from competitive football showed on the field. Despite the straight year of daily training in Bloomington, Florida, and now Los Angeles, there was much more to do and learn.

I remember being on the phone pleading with the assistant couch to give me a chance to get better. I'll never forget what he said to me. He said that I had a great deal of will, but my quickness, speed and coordination was the worst he'd probably ever seen in his life. He said that he, a man in his late thirties, early forties, had a better chance of making the team, and that I should not waste my time, and to find something else to do with my life.

He was so blunt with me, but I did not let his negative words sink inside my mind. I thanked him for his honesty and the opportunity to tryout. The moment I hung up the phone, the fire in my heart was magnified! I knew who I was! I did not know how I would achieve the dreams that God had put in my heart, but I was convinced more than ever before, that they would somehow, someway, come to pass! Instead of giving up, packing my possessions, and leaving Los Angeles, I continued training with Peyton.

I thought to myself, "I have an entire year to train and try out again for the team."

Training with Peyton was very inspiring. Through him, I met the former Olympic world record holder in the 100 meter dash. I could remember being about 14 years old and reading about him in a magazine at my high school cafeteria, and now, more than 7 years later, I was on the same track with him. Things like that are just surreal. Another day, I would meet another womens' record holder in the 200 meter dash, Alyson Felix. Just about 4 years before, when I had just moved in to my dorm room as a freshman at Indiana University, I sat on my bed reading about and admiring her in a magazine. I would never have dreamed at the time, that I would ever meet these inspirations in my lifetime. Only Christ can architect these divine connections!

Slowly but surely, I was beginning to be surrounded by the right people. I was beginning to see with my own eyes, all the possibilities of Jesus. I recall standing there on the track, under the hot sun, asking Maurice Green questions about how to get faster. I had the physique. I had the will. However, I just could not lower my speed time.

After a while, Maurice Green spoke about nutrition. He recommended his nutritionist, Chase Thomas, the same nutritionist that Peyton had recommended I speak to previously. Chase's office and store was just five minutes away from the track. Now that I had a second recommendation, especially from the world record holder, I knew that I had to go and see him.

My journey continued. So one afternoon, a few days later, I went in to speak with Chase Thomas for just a few minutes. That few minutes turned into more than an hour in his office as I soaked in all the waves of nutritional knowledge and wisdom that he was showering upon me. That one meeting completely changed my life and the way that I looked at my body, health, and nutrition. Chase set me on a journey towards a healthier lifestyle.

Chapter 8

It was about a week after being cut from the football team, when I was walking down the famous Wilshire Boulevard on my way from an internet cafe in Koreatown. I had on my typical tank top, pants, and sandals that hot Los Angeles afternoon. I was walking into a nearby Verizon mobile phone store to replace a charger that suddenly had stopped working a few days before.

As I walked into the store, I saw an African American man sitting at the table outside the coffee shop, adjacent to the store. He was looking into my direction. As always, I returned a smile, nodded my head, and walked into the store.

A while later, as I was exiting the store, the man said "hello" and introduced himself to me. His name was Eli White. He was a noted photographer. He told me how beautiful and unique he thought I was, and asked me if I ever modeled before. I told him that I had just done my first photo shoot a few weeks before, but that I was there in LA to focus on football. We spoke for some time, and before I left, he reached into his shoulder bag and pulled out a few samples of his work with his contact information on them. I remember looking at his work of the male models that he had shot. And to be honest, I was not impressed. It was art modeling photographs, some in color and some in black and white. I was not interested in any types of modeling besides high fashion. How naive time would have eventually proved me to be. My mind had yet to be expanded.

Months must have gone by with his photographs sitting in the bottom of my suitcase in my bedroom. I even recall seeing him on the bus late one night, after returning from training with Peyton. I must have been less than a few feet away from him, however, I did not say a word to Eli, as I exited the bus. I was hoping that he had not noticed me. I acted as if I hadn't noticed him. I had far too much on my mind to be worrying about modeling at that point. I was diligently trying to get faster on the track. I was selling pills to clients in LA and all over the country. I had my love, Taylor, in Florida, and I was running businesses online, trying to make sure that my rent and bills were paid on time. Modeling would surely have to wait.

My daily routine continued – socializing, selling herbals, training, and online business. I had kept in contact with my former love and still best friend, Stella the entire time.

Soon, I was paying for a ticket for her to come and visit me from Indiana. She didn't believe me. Coming to Los Angeles was a dream of hers. I had always promised her that I would love her forever, and that I would do such things for her in the future.

The future was here. I missed her so much. It was tearing my heart apart to be away from my best friend. The feeling was mutual. She was ecstatic to see me in Los Angeles.

Conveniently, around the same time, my girlfriend Taylor and I were going through some difficulties. We missed each other so much, that we would get extremely frustrated each time we spoke on the phone.

After many frustrating conversations with my princess, Taylor, I decided that we needed to take a break from one another. She was not happy, but neither was I. However, perhaps, I knew in the back of my mind that I would be flying my former love, Stella over.

I was a changed man as far as relationships went. I would feel terrible if I would have had sex with Stella, while Taylor was under the impression that we were still together.

Had it been just a year before, with my old, sly ways, I wouldn't have thought twice about being unfaithful.

Nevertheless, as the days until Stella's flight approached, I began to have second thoughts about sleeping with Stella when she arrived. During a conversation on the phone one day, I told her that I had something to tell her. I told her that maybe we shouldn't continue to talk sexually to one another on the phone, and that I didn't think that we should have sex when she arrived.

Needless to say, Stella was not happy at all. At first, she thought that I was joking, but as I continued to insist, she realized that I was being serious. My heart was still in Florida with my princess, Taylor. I could not get her off my mind. She was now my future.

I remember coming from football practice and seeing Stella with her luggage, waiting for me in my apartment. My apartment manager had let her in. I smiled and shook my head. She smiled back. The feelings rushed back to my heart immediately. I was looking into the eyes of my best friend in the entire world and my love. This was the girl that knew me more than any girl did. This was the girl that bailed me out when I needed her most. It had been about six whole months since the last day that I had seen her face, smelled her scent, or touched her skin. This was my college love!

We had never been apart for that long, since we met each other that night, during my freshman year in college, four years before. Stella looked absolutely radiant in my eyes. We hugged for what seemed to be an eternity.

"How" I thought to myself, "Am I going to resist making love to her?"

Later that night in bed with Stella, after returning home from a night out, with a few drinks in our system, Stella and I under the covers, we got very close to one another. Articles of clothing started coming off. But just when we were going to make love, I stopped. Taylor would just not leave my mind.

"I can't do this." I said to Stella.

She could not believe that I had led her on. She was not happy at all. Soon, tears began rolling down from Stella's eyes. I laugh now, because Stella, knowing me more than any other girl in the world, knew my weakness. I could not stand to be the cause of a girl crying.

That night, we made deep, endless love until the sun came up. Stella's trip to visit me turned out to be a dream visit for the both of us. For the first time, away from the hectic college environment, I could see Stella as my only woman.

For over a week, we were inseparable. Yet, it was sad to know that within a blink of an eye, she would be going back to Indiana.

I watched sadly, as she went away to the airport in the taxi, knowing that there was a good possibility that I would not see her again. Good bye my lover. Good bye forever.

For about a week, however, we continued to have romantic late night conversations on the phone. We were going to give our long distance love a chance. However, we were just not meant to be more than just friends. One conversation, I was telling her that I had been thinking of Taylor. And I lied and told her that I had sex with a girl in Los Angeles after a night out.

Another conversation, she was telling me that she had sex with a former high school boyfriend. On the phone with her, I acted as if I was hurt and devastated, but truly, I was looking for an excuse to put a close to our intimacy. I told her that it would be best if we just remained friends.

By the grace of God, the separation and break from my princess, Taylor only made our love intensify. I could tell by the sweet sound of Taylor's voice after I called her for the first time in weeks, that she dearly missed me. I dearly missed her too. We were back on the path of love! Taylor was my true love, and now I was sure!

Chapter 9

Over the course of the next few months, our love was truly put to the test by the distance of our spirits. I spent countless lonely nights on the phone with her, whispering sweet nothings into her ears, consoling her, letting her know that we would soon be together once again.

Many a night, we stared at the bright full moon from opposite ends of the country. We dreamed of one another constantly. Our loving hearts and souls were in sync. The thought of her, sent chills up and down my body.

Valentine's Day came and went. I sent her cards and a pink, ruby and diamond heart necklace to signify my love for her. I wanted to spoil my princess more. If there was any doubt as to whether I had fallen head over heels in love with this princess from Florida, then the time she was not able to visit me during her spring recess of her final year in college would wipe away any doubts.

Even now, years later, writing about my past lovers, Stella and Taylor, and listing to love songs, makes me sure and confident that somewhere out there, waiting to be discovered, is the true, divine love of my life, dreaming, fantasizing, believing for me to come and sweep her completely off her feet.

To her I say, "I'm coming in due time! Wait patiently my love…! I'm coming…! We shall soon meet one another on the journey to The Kingdom of Heaven!"

Taylor and I had built up much anticipation to finally see one another after so many months. Her spring recess allowed us the chance for our hearts to finally unite again.

Since my father worked for the airlines, he was able to book Taylor a flight from Florida to California for about $100 dollars. Each waking day that approached her flight made our hearts yearn to touch one another. My love was coming to me! The days seemed to slow. The anticipation heightened! We needed each other. Our love was mad and intense! For the first time in my young life, I was experiencing a heightened state of love and desire. It was such a surreal feeling.

Finally, the day had arrived for my sweetheart to come. I was thrilled beyond words. There were fireworks in my body. I was filled with glee! There was absolutely nothing in the entire world that could bring me down from the euphoric high that I was experiencing!

Because we had booked the plane ticket through my father, her flight was on standby. That meant that she did not have a guaranteed flight. She would be allowed to board the plane only if there were extra available seats on the plane.

I was not too worried though. I remained optimistic. I believe that we booked the flight on a weekday that was not a busy traveling day. Plus, we booked the earliest flight that we could find. We did not want to take any chances.

Taylor arrived at the airport at dusk, before the rise of the sun. She called me as I slept deeply in Los Angeles, a three hour time difference from Florida time. My soul sang, hearing the voice of my princess, who would soon be at my side once again. I stayed on the phone with her as the flight boarded.

"Oh, no!" I thought to myself some time later.

The final passenger had boarded the airplane, and there was no vacant seat for my love to board. My heart sank. But I tried to remain optimistic.

"It's ok." I assured Taylor, my darling, "You'll get on the next flight, love."

About an hour or two later, Taylor called me. I waited optimistically on the phone with her, hoping that she would be able to board the flight. Once again, unfortunately, the plane was full of paying passengers and standby passengers who had priority over her. My heart sank once again. The odds of us seeing one another were weighing against us.

"It's ok baby." I comforted her, "You'll get on the next flight."

For the remainder of the now, long day, one flight after another departed without my love on board. I was devastated! Morning turned to noon. Noon turned to afternoon. And then, afternoon turned to evening. That day, I felt an agonizing and burning pain in my heart that I had never felt before. My mind ran wild. It had been almost a year since I had seen my darling princess. I had stored up in me so much emotion in my heart to see her, and now, it seemed that it was not meant to be.

Driving through Los Angeles traffic in my car, later that evening, with my heart ever aching to see Taylor, we comforted one another on the phone, desperately struggling to remain positive and to find a solution to our dire dilemma. I even offered to pay for an expensive ticket for her to arrive the next morning. She declined however, wanting me to save my money. I yearned to see her badly, and I was willing to do anything in the world at that point!

That trying day was the day! That was the moment that I knew in my heart that I was absolutely in love with this woman. Never had I felt the way that I felt in that car! Never had I pained so much from not being able to see another human being! I now knew that she was the one and only for me.

Taylor never boarded the plane that evening. After two long days of trying to unite, Taylor and I finally conceded to the fact that we should wait until she graduated university in a few months before reuniting. I recall now, thinking that there was absolutely no way in the world that my soul could go on for that long without feeling her touch, without smelling her scent, without kissing her sweet honey lips. It was going to be a great challenge for me.

Perhaps, it was good that she did not come. I had to remain completely focused on all the varying dimensions that I was in.

Not long after, my wealth began to rapidly multiply. I was introduced to drug dealers who instantly became great friends. They were some of the most amazing human beings in the world. You would never think, if you saw them in the street, that they were drug dealers. I remained fortunate and guarded in the eyes of the Lord. Still, I was surrounded by goodness, despite my infirmities and transgressions. Why? Because of His endless love!

More clients who had heard of me were flying in to Los Angeles to do business with me. I was living my dream. I had the love of my life and I was a drug lord!

I had been working nonstop for months now, training, modeling and doing business along with other ventures. I needed a break from the fast life. I needed a break from this movie that I was living. I missed all my best friends from Indiana University. I missed Stella. I missed Landon. I missed Gavin.

I flew back to Bloomington for a few days to get my mind humbled and grounded again. I was back in my paradise cluster of a town. It was absolutely refreshing to see all my old friends again. I had been away for so long. It seemed like an eternity. The emotions were still there between Stella and me. This time however, she had a boyfriend that she seemed to be in love with. I was happy that she was happy. It was good to be with Stella again. A few times during the vacation, we came awfully close to becoming intimate again; however, I think we both knew that it would be best not to do that to one another, as well as our new loves.

That chapter of our love life ended on that visit. There was finally closure to our long adventurous journey of infatuation. We kissed our last kiss after she drove me to the airport. We both had a sense that this was it. I boarded the plane back to Los Angeles, and to this day, although Stella and I still love one another and keep touch, we have yet to meet face to face again.

Chapter 10

It was back to LA to my fast moving exciting life! The seasons changed. Finally, the love of my life, Taylor had graduated and received a degree in architecture. She sold most of her possessions, packed her luggage, leaving everything that she knew and loved behind in Florida to come to me in Los Angeles.

My nerves ran wild the weeks prior, knowing that she would be coming to live with me. I had never permanently lived with a girlfriend before. I had no idea how good or bad it would be. It was one thing to be in love with a woman, but another thing to live with one. I had second thoughts, but in the end, as always, love won the battle.

In my red convertible classic BMW that I had recently bought, a freshly shaved bald head, and the biggest smile on my face, I drove to LAX airport to pick up and see my princess for the first time in such a long time.

I could not believe that our hearts had made it apart for so long. It is astonishing what true love can do with time and thoughts. At the airport terminal, with her luggage on the ground at her side, we stood there hugging for an eternity.

Ah…mi amor!

The moment I laid eyes on her, all my cares disappeared! The wait was all well worth it. We did not want to let each other out of our arms. Fate had separated us for too long. We held hands tightly the entire ride as I drove us back home.

I felt butterflies in my chest the entire time. It was as if, if we let go, she would vanish back to Florida. We could not believe that it was true. I could not believe that she was actually in LA.

I can never forget that night. We made passionate love all night long under the bright moon's sky. Time passed by. It was an amazing and interesting experience living with Taylor. Our love only grew stronger and richer each passing day.

Looking back, I recall stopping my dealings when she came. I did not want to put my dove into danger like I had lived through in the past. It was not worth it. My other ventures, like modeling and business seemed to have slowed as well. It was in no way Taylor's fault, but perhaps, at the tender age of 22 years old, I was ill-prepared for a woman in my life.

However, it was truly a fairy tale beginning, living with my princess. We took many a long walks on the beach. We went out to celebrity events and nightclubs together. We dined at fancy restaurants. We laughed. We danced. We fought. We loved. The entire time, our love for one another was magnifying!

Before Taylor came to Los Angeles, I had told her that Stella had come to visit me. Understandably, she did not feel comfortable living in my apartment in Koreatown. It was time to move once more. I too was ready for a change, a fresh start once more. We looked for many apartments in luxurious Beverly Hills, Santa Monica, and Malibu, and even considered buying a home together. However, we were turned down many times because we did not have much established combined credit.

I'm always thankful that Christ did not allow us to commit to buying a home, considering what lay just ahead of us in the world. Jesus has always had a remarkable way of protecting His child and keeping me out of dangerous roads.

By this time, months had gone by since Taylor had arrived. It made me sad to see my princess go through the uncertainty that I went through the first time that I arrived in Los Angeles. She contemplated giving up and returning back home to Florida. I did my best to encourage and assure her that through Christ and the power of believing in Him, we would surely find a place, despite this seemingly hopeless circumstance we were facing.

By this point, I knew and was beginning to understand the Power that I had with me.

"Trust me Taylor..." I recall assuring her many days.

I should have been saying, "Trust in Jesus."

After about a month of continuous, daily ordeal in finding a new place, at last, the day had come that an apartment complex was willing to let us dwell there! Not only was it in an ideal location. And not only was it a luxurious abode, but it was the Villa Azure, the spectacular Mexican resort style apartment complex with hot tubs, waterfalls cascading down boulders, palm trees with humming birds nestled in them and so much more beauties, that I had promised myself that I would live there about a year before!

It was the same complex that I met the photographer, Zachary, who discovered me, and had the group of models surrounding the entrance!

Just as I had envisioned and believed wholeheartedly to live in The Boulders, back in Bloomington, Indiana, while living in the homeless shelter, I had envisioned and believed wholeheartedly that I would surely, by the grace and divine favor of Jesus, live in the heavenly Villa Azure estates!

Now, once again, my dream had become a reality! More and more, I was understanding that I was a blessed man indeed!

After we became settled in our new luxury condominium, Taylor found a job in a boutique, high end clothing store in Santa Monica, while she searched for a permanent job as an architect.

Meanwhile, I was living off of my savings, while searching and believing for the next big opportunity that Christ had in store for me.

Time continued to pass by, and I was making nowhere near the money that I was making before Taylor arrived in LA. For me, that was not a problem. I knew that with much patience and persistence, my breakthrough would come again.

However, for Taylor, a woman that had been used to the normal structure of doing things all her life, she could not understand the season of planting seeds and patience that I was in.

After a few rejections in modeling, and ideas that did not immediately yield profits, she wanted me to find a normal job as she was doing. There was no way that I was willing to do so. It was just too much for her, or any other woman to handle. And I understood that. The month to month life of barely getting by was certainly not what my princess had in mind before coming to me. She deserved better. She deserved more.

Then one day, I got an email offering me up to $200 dollars of credit to gamble online if I started with my own $200 dollars. At the time, it was a eureka moment! It was exactly what I was waiting for. It had been five long years since I had gambled in high school. Online gambling was legal at the time, not that it would have mattered if it wasn't.

So after a few days of carefully thinking about it, I decided to invest $200 dollars, which gave me $400 dollars in the casino account after the matching bonus.

"This is too good to be true!" I thought.

It's not every day that a company, or anyone for that matter, gives you $200 dollars, free of charge. But at the same time, I was well aware of the tactic casinos used to suck people into losing all their money. I had been gambling for far too long not to be aware.

I had to mentally prepare my mind for the path that I was about to embark on. At first, I did not tell Taylor that I was gambling online. I knew that she would not understand nor approve.

Within days of patiently playing the card game, blackjack online, I had made a few hundred dollars.

Of course, my mind went wild, thinking about how easy it was to make that amount of money legally, in such a small time frame.

Immediately, I started doing the math in my head, thinking, naively, that I could, and would do it for the rest of my life. I cashed out my winnings the moment that I was ahead, just like I had done to my frustrated friends while gambling in school many years before. I was ecstatic inside!

The next phase was to see if the company would mail me a check of my winnings. To my surprise, the check came in the mail about a week later.

The final phase was to wait about two weeks to see whether or not the check would default in the bank. To my surprise again, the check was authentic.

The trial period was complete! It gave me the green light to think bigger! I used the money to pay off some minor bills and debts, and the rest of the money to gamble with again.

Finally, I told Taylor about my new venture. Reluctantly, she allowed me to continue. She was not exactly happy with the idea, however, as long as I was finally generating some kind of income to contribute to the relationship, she was not going to force me to stop, despite her reservations about gambling.

I lost a few hundred dollars the next time. I had no money in my bank account that night to continue, and everyone who has gambled before, knows the anxious feeling inside to continue when you are down.

I used $500 dollars out of my princess, Taylor's account. She was visiting her family in Florida that week. Now, I knew that I had to win in order to avoid damaging our relationship upon her return.

Also, I told myself that I could always sell one of my luxury possessions if I lost the $500 dollars.

From the moment I deposited the money into my casino account, I tuned my mind to utter focus. I put aside all of my emotions. If it were my money, I would be much upset by loosing, but when it comes to money of others, I am 1000% focused.

I convinced myself that this was only a computer with a simple recipe – an algorithm. Computers have been around for but a few years, while the human brain has been evolving for billions and billions of years and more.

I told myself that it would be most likely illegal for a casino to design a game that made the players lose more than 25% of the time if they played conservatively. After I had accepted this belief, I was ready to go into my own world – Maubrey's world!

$500 dollars turned to $600 dollars. $600 dollars turned to $700 dollars. $700 dollars turned to $800 dollars. By the end of the evening, after a few hours of complete discipline and focus, I had accumulated over $1000 dollars! I now thought of it as a regular job.

With over $500 dollars profit in a few hours, I thought to myself that I was making over $250 dollars per hour. That night, I went to sleep very happy and excited...more than usual.

Over the course of the following month or so, my routine was to wake up, drive Taylor to work in Santa Monica, and then race back in my red BMW convertible to the computer in my pajamas, and then gamble online while eating breakfast.

I still remember the high rush that I would get in my body whenever I would win a large amount of money. Alone in our apartment, I would be jumping high in the air in celebration.

Sometimes, I would gamble online for a few hours and make a few hundred dollars. Sometimes I would make over $2000 dollars in a few minutes then go and relax in our apartment complex's pool and hot tub.

Other days, I would go shopping. After I picked my princess up in the evening, sometimes, I would take her out to fancy restaurants. I was living a dream! I was back in my zone! I had figured out the recipe. I had cracked the code!

At times, I even wondered if the company would send someone to kill me for winning all that money. But then I realized that for the large amount of money that I was winning daily, there were probably hundreds of millions of dollars being lost by other gamblers who were not as focused, disciplined, and fortunate as I was.

Some days, I lost money, most days I won large bulks of money. Starting with only $500 dollars that I had borrowed from Taylor's account, within a very short time, I had suddenly amassed over $32,000 dollars! I started dreaming of all my plans that I had dreamed in the past of investing in. I thought of investing in luxury real estate, jewelry, and cars. Now, my eyes were on winning $50,000 dollars, then $100,000 dollars.

Soon, I let my emotions consume me and began diverting from my master plan. Soon, I began losing thousands of dollars. I had to get back to focus. I envisioned losing all that money that I had spent so much time, energy and effort to obtain.

I got a flashback of when I was in high school and lost not nearly as much as $32,000 dollars, but close to a thousand dollars one spring, after going on a long winning streak. I immediately regained my calm and composure, and then started using my proven method again.

In the end, I had won about $28,000 dollars in a little over a month, a profit of about 6000%! Through it all, I lost my darling princess, Taylor, because of the down days and disagreements on how to use the winnings.

Also, there she was, going to work, and working hard for over nine hours almost every day, and here I was, spending but a few moments on the computer and making a monthly salary in just a few minutes.

I'll never forget the day, and the look on her face, when I nervously told her that I had lost over a thousand dollars one day in a restaurant in Santa Monica, after picking her up from work.

"That's it, Maubrey!" she said, "I'm leaving you."

I sat there speechless. I couldn't say a thing. She had warned me many times before. I knew that she did not deserve going through the ups and downs of my financials.

To me, it was absolutely a norm. But for her, and most women, it was unfathomable. I could not blame her.

For the next few months, still living together, I tried everything in my power to win her love back. I humbled myself towards her; I sang sweet songs to her in the mornings in bed. I gave her foot massages. I cooked gourmet meals for her. I sent her love text messages while she was at work. Anything sweet that I could think of, I would do for my love.

It seemed, after a while, that she was changing her mind about leaving me and returning back to Florida. I couldn't imagine life without my princess. We had made so many promises to each other. We had made passionate, sweet love so many nights. We had stared deeply into the eyes of one another and saw the universe and our future.

Day after day, after much effort on my part, it seemed as if our hearts were uniting again. I thought that I had suffered long enough. But alas, after one more fight about how we should spend the final, over $5,000 dollar check that came in the mail from the casino company, she moved out to a co-workers apartment that afternoon.

I can still remember how loudly she screamed and yelled at me in our condo, that sunny afternoon, and me finally losing my calm, and shouting at her to "just leave" if she wanted to.

Shortly later, she was in our condo with a co-worker helping her pack her possessions. At first, I was happy and relieved that she was out of my life. I felt free! I felt liberated!

But then, after only a week, my heart burned for her love and touch. I promised myself not to call her. But I called.

When we spoke, she felt the same way about me. Our love was just too strong to be extinguished because of money. Again, over the phone this time, we got closer and closer.

Perhaps, our hearts were better off loving from afar. I had dreamed and hoped that after a short time of living apart from one another, that my darling lover would eventually return to me.

Once more, I was wrong. She had set a date to leave Los Angeles in the upcoming weeks. The news was like a dagger in my already aching heart! My world shattered, as I sat there all alone in my bedroom as she broke the saddening news to me!

I went many sleepless nights thinking about my love. I fought to the very end to convince her to stay.

I had sold my red BMW convertible in the midst of all my gambling days. So weeks before Taylor left, we were struggling with no car. I am certain that, although she said that she loved me without the car, that it made her decision about leaving much easier.

A few weeks after my love had moved out. I bought a more updated, black BMW. What a day that was for me. It seemed that I had all that I wanted; the car, the home, the clothes, the jewelry, but no princess to share it with.

During our telephone conversations the weeks leading to her departure from LA, I saw that she was struggling without a car. I could not bear to know that my love was out there in the middle of LA, on her own, without a car. The Lord spoke to me in my sleep one night.

He said, "Give Taylor the car."

So, one day, as hard as it was for me to do, and after days of thinking about it, I called my love and told her that I wanted to give her the black BMW that I had just recently bought.

She seemed stunned on the phone, perhaps, thinking that it was too good to be true. It didn't make sense to me either. She felt that she deserved it though. But up to that date, it was the biggest gift that I had ever given a woman, or anyone in my life.

However, in my heart, she was my princess still, the beautiful girl I had met that one fateful night in Tallahassee, Florida. The girl that I tried to kiss and was rejected in the parking lot that first night after the nightclub. My love divine!

Perhaps, a part of me hoped that giving Taylor my BMW would make her stay. If so, then I was wrong about love once again. She used the car for a few weeks, and then sold it just before leaving Los Angeles, never to return to me again.

How sad this seemingly perfect fairy tale love story abruptly ended. In no way however, do I blame my princess for leaving. I forced her to leave. A woman would have to be absolutely crazy, or absolutely crazy in love, to stay with me through those obstacles and circumstances.

But knowing all that I had overcome in my past, most of which I kept away from her, all I wanted was to find the woman that was extremely patient, crazy enough, and had a crystal clear foresight about my glorious future to stand confidently by my side through the storm and fire, before the time of harvest and abundance came.

There are over 6,800,000,000 billion beings in the world as we know. Perhaps, there is but one woman alive or yet to be born that is for me.

The irony of the story is that, I had the ability to save our relationship. All I had to do was to listen to Taylor and put my grand dreams on hold and find a normal job, and do things and behave like normal people do.

But there is a problem. I am not a normal person. I have never been a normal person. I had heard Taylor's suggestion many times from friends and family who had my best interest in heart, but there has always been a burning fire in my heart to never give up or settle!

Plus, I vividly recall, during one of our phone conversations, as I begged her to stay and try to work out the relationship, when she said that it wouldn't work because,

"You were never going to marry me anyway."

"I will!" I replied.

But she was not convinced. She was ready to get married, have children with me, and buy a home together. And me, being a year younger than she was, and only 22 years old, I was not ready for the commitment or the responsibility yet. I had to be absolutely sure first.

After being deeply in love with Stella for four whole years in Indiana, and then having a change of heart, I realized that I did not know everything about love. I wanted to take my time before making a commitment.

The old Maubrey would have lied and told Taylor whatever she wanted to hear. The new, more compassionate and honest Maubrey was more upfront and truthful, despite the outcome. I was now aware that my heart could change in the future. In the back of my mind though, I pictured us spending eternity together. Perhaps, Taylor didn't realize that. She wanted to hear me say the words. I felt that she was my all! I just was not willing to make any promises to her.

Taylor was absolutely in love with me, as I was with her, but there seemed to be no way that it would work between us. My fairy tale princess was now out of my life!

The irony was that just a few weeks after I had received my last check from the casino, and after Taylor had left me, President Bush signed a law making online gambling illegal. The Lord Jesus had architected the series of events perfectly, in His divine order. What was meant to be, was exactly as it happened.

Only Christ knows what, or who else in my life I would have lost as a result of gambling! What a learning experience that was for me!

Chapter 11

When Taylor left LA, it was a new beginning for me. I felt like a new and refreshed man. I became more social. I became more focused. Still, it seemed like every song on the radio reminded me of my darling princess. I missed her dearly, but as hard as it was, I had to move on with my life. I had to let her go.

About a month after Taylor had left, my brother thought it would be a good idea for me to meet him in Las Vegas for my 23rd birthday weekend, to take my mind off of my love.

At first, I was hesitant. I was never one to take vacations or breaks, but after some persuasion on his part, I agreed. This was going to be my first time going to Las Vegas! Also, it had been over a year since I had seen my dear brother. I missed him much. I was excited! I packed up a suitcase and took a bus to Las Vegas the next morning.

Las Vegas!

I lost $100 dollars that my brother had given me to gamble within only two minutes. That was it for me, as far as gambling in casinos. This was certainly not like any online gambling.

I had so much to drink later that night. My brother was buying me drinks. Strangers bought me drinks. Women bought me drinks. The next thing I know, I was separated from my brother and ended up joining a random group of other party people, going from different nightclub to nightclub. I only remember them treating me with much love and buying me drink after drink. There was much dancing and celebrating that night.

By the time I had realized it. It was morning, the sun was coming up, and I had no battery life in my phone. I did not know my brother's phone number by heart. I returned to the lobby of Caesar's Palace alone with no idea of how to get to the house, a few miles off the Vegas strip that my brother and I were to be staying. After wondering around the casino lobby for some time, exhausted, hungry and extremely intoxicated, I looked at the casinos carpeted floor, looked around, looked back at the floor, looked around again, then decided to just fall asleep right there on the floor early that morning.

I must have woke up about an hour later to the tap of a security guard telling me that I could not sleep on the floor. I imagine I wasn't the first one to fall asleep right on the casino floor.

Finally, somehow, I was able to reach my brother on the phone. He was extremely worried and concerned for my safety. Earlier, a casino security guard told me that my brother had been frantically searching for me, practically in tears.

Yes, I knew that my brother loved me with all his heart. He would not be able to bare, knowing that he had brought his younger brother to Las Vegas, and have something bad happen to me. I could hear the sound of relief when he heard the sound of my voice. I told him where to pick me up.

While I waited, all my best friends from Indiana called to wish me happy birthday. My love, Taylor called too! Talking to her brought back my love for her. I could tell by our conversation, that she was still in love with me too. I missed her even more.

My brother finally drove to pick me up and took me to the friend's house that we were visiting.

Vegas was such a wild experience! Later that evening, one of my old high school friends surprised me for my birthday and appeared out of nowhere, all the way from New Jersey.

Another day, my brother's friend that we were staying with, drove home extremely drunk early one morning, made it safely all the way from the casinos, and then completely wrecked his car as well as a parked car, just blocks from his home.

I recall being suddenly awakened by him storming into the house, his eyes blurred and diluted, in a frantic panic, telling me that he just got into a major car wreck. He had driven away from the wreck as quickly as he could, knowing that if the police were called, he would surely be arrested for drunk driving.

I remember him asking me to come with him to the scene of the accident just blocks away. The parked car was completely destroyed! He had rushed back home to hide his damaged car in the garage.

A few minutes later, as he was describing his outrageous night to us, we heard the doorbell ring. It was the father and family of the teenager whose car had been wrecked. It seems that they circled the area and followed the trail straight to the house. Plus, I believe our friend's license plate had been stuck to the teenager's car during the wreck.

If I thought life in Los Angeles was insane, then it was nothing, compared to my short, three day visit to Las Vegas!

Then, just hours later, I found myself upstairs in the room of our friend's female roommate, talking about sex as she showed me nude photos of her on her website. A few minutes later, I was taking sexual photos of her outside the house in the middle of the street.

I thought to myself, "This city is crazy!"

It is no wonder that Las Vegas is called "Sin City".

The sex.
The drugs.
The alcohol.
The money!

What a dizzying adventure that was for me. My old friend from high school and I took a road trip back to Los Angeles from Las Vegas together. I showed him my beautiful home. I had come a long way from the ghettos of Irvington, New Jersey where we attended high school together. He was extremely impressed and proud of me. He stayed for two days. I showed him around town, took him to nightclubs and restaurants, and introduced him to a few of my friends.

After he left, it was back to focus. The party was over. I had to dig deep to figure out how I was going to continue paying for my lavish lifestyle. The rent and bills were rapidly pilling up. I had to think at an accelerated pace.

After days of pondering and brainstorming, I decided to go back to dealing! I told myself that I would only deal the herbal pills and marijuana. I knew that the laws in California concerning marijuana were lax. Still, I was going to use all that I had learned from my case in Bloomington, Indiana, to avoid getting caught.

The danger of selling in Los Angeles still was the least of my worries. If anything, I had become more fearless and confident in dealing drugs. So after all that Jesus had brought me out of, foolishly and desperately, I decided to buy a bulk amount of marijuana again! I was really testing my Lord!

I remember the day clearly. I had thousands of dollars worth of herbal ecstasy pills and a postal money order of over $2,000 dollars to pay for my past due rent. I had a big decision to make. I could use the money order to pay my past due rent and avoid possible eviction, or I could take a big risk and invest it on buying a large amount of marijuana.

The moment I bought the marijuana, the clock would start ticking until the time I would be evicted and homeless again. I really dug deep in my soul that day.

I told myself, "Maubrey, you are all powerful! You can sell water to a well…ice to an Eskimo. You can do anything!"

At that instant, I had convinced myself! My mind was set! I got on the phone and called everyone I could think about, who would have or know someone who had that amount of marijuana. I needed pounds! I had no success in finding someone in Los Angeles. Marijuana was not my specialty. The herbal pills were, so I had no connections to Marijuana.

After more thinking, I called one of my good friends from New Jersey and asked him if any of his friends in LA knew someone who could sell me that amount. He did!

Before I knew it, I was being picked up in a car by Nigerian rappers, en route to meet the supplier. It was in the middle of a hot California day. Three cars pulled up into an open parking lot. I guess we were all worried more about being ripped off or shot at, than being arrested by the police.

Once again, I felt like I was in a movie scene. To my surprise, the supplier was a woman – a petite, Asian woman. More than ever now, I felt as if I were in a movie.

"Only you!" she exclaimed.

She only wanted me to enter the car with her. We drove to the other end of the huge parking lot.

"You're not a cop are you?" she asked me in her deep Asian accent, as she frisked my body.

"No. Are you?" I replied.

I couldn't help but laugh inside, as she lifted her shirt to show that she wasn't wearing a recording device, revealing her firm breasts.

"This woman is quite an animated character!" I thought to myself.

I liked her energy. She showed me the marijuana. I showed her the money order. She wasn't very happy to see that I did not have cash. She thought I might be wasting her time or attempting to rob her or scam her with a counterfeit money order. I told her that the check was for my rent and that I wasn't sure if I was going to be robbed too, which was the reason I brought the check.

I let her know that now that I trusted her, I would cash the check and meet her the next day. Reluctantly, she seemed to believe me. She liked my energy. We exchanged contact information. She gave me about $100 dollars worth of a sample of marijuana for my new Nigerian friends to try, since I didn't smoke.

We got back to my apartment. The Nigerians smoked a sample. They loved it! We spoke and joked for a few hours in my apartment, then said goodbye.

Early the next day, the check was cashed. I bought a pound of marijuana from my new Asian female friend. Her husband was in the back seat counting the cash, while I was examining and weighing the marijuana. Everything looked good. The deal was made.

I thought to myself, "This could be the beginning of a good friendship!"

I knew, from the many years of dealing, how hard it was to find honest partners. She told of how there was something about me that she trusted, that I gave off a good vibe. I thanked her and told her that I felt the same way about her. We were rebellious and breaking the law, but it is amazing how the Lord can bring divine connections under the most unlikely circumstances.

She even went out of her way and drove me about an hour home through Los Angeles traffic, since I did not have a car, something she said she had never done for a customer before. I thanked her, gave her a hug and exited the SUV when we arrived at The Villa Azure.

I remember walking through the gates of my apartment complex's pool area, extremely excited inside, with the strong aroma of marijuana ascending from my backpack. When I got to my apartment, I was still nervous that the DEA could come storming in at anytime, however I quickly tuned the negative thoughts out of my mind and got straight to work.

Chapter 12

It had been many, many years, after getting arrested my second year in Bloomington, since I had handled marijuana, but surely, my old routine of weighing and bagging the marijuana all came back to me.

I sent a mass text message that I was in business, put in the rap artist, Young Jeezy's CD, who I had listened to non-stop, while dealing in Bloomington, Indiana, Florida, and the early months of dealing in California.

I could relate to all the lyrics in his songs, almost like he had a hidden camera on me and was speaking about my life as a dealer. I would be listening to his music on replay for many months after that afternoon.

When customers came to my apartment to make a purchase, all they would hear was Young Jeezy's music playing, fortissimo, in the background. Not only did Young Jeezy's music inspire and motivate me to be fearless, but incase a client was working for the DEA and wearing a recording device, they would not be able to hear my voice.

Within a few weeks, I had sold out the entire pound of marijuana, paid my past due rent, and was back to having positive cash-flow!

I became a networking machine, a super socialite! I would talk to absolutely everybody that I met in my resort-like apartment complex. I would talk to everyone that I met in Los Angeles. My phone list of clientele soared! Between the herbal pills and marijuana alone, I was making thousands of dollars a week! This time, I did not bother to buy another car. I had drivers that trafficked the marijuana to me, eliminating my risk. I had a sense that now, I was closely been watched by the DEA and possibly the FBI, waiting for me to make a mistake.

In the evenings, I would call my celebrity limousine driver to pick me up and chauffeur me to the nightclubs. Life was fantastic! Like a dream. I had all the friends in the world. Everyone knew me. My clients seemed to be all genuine towards me. No longer was I sad about losing Taylor.

Yet, I was still lacking one thing, the thing that I had journeyed to Los Angeles for – to get fast enough to become a professional football player. Through all my ups and downs, I had not given up on the dream! As it had happened many times in the past, this time, I wanted to make sure that the lack of financial freedom would never again get in my way and prevent me from achieving my dreams.

Foolishly, this was the best way I knew how to get where I wanted to be. After just a few months, despite having over $50,000 dollars worth of product by then, the money was never enough to stop. The more money I made, the more I thought I could reinvest. It was a nonstop cycle. I didn't buy anything fancy, I never overspent. I just kept reinvesting. I wanted to get the most out of my money so that I could stop selling as fast as possible and focus on my true dreams.

Then one day, my online herbal pill supplier, who I spoke about in my earlier writings, suddenly said that she would not be selling the pills anymore. Only now, over three years later, is the true reason revealed.

So, for the following weeks, I sold only marijuana. The money began to slow. My bills and expenses began to pile.

Then one day, a customer offered to pay for my marijuana for a few genuine ecstasy pills. Hesitantly, I agreed. Now, for the first time, since Christ had delivered me from spending 60 years in prison, I was in possession of ecstasy, MDNA again!

After all the prayers, after all the tears, after all that I had put my family and close friends through, foolishly and selfishly, I went back to that world!

Selling marijuana, was illegal, however, in California, I would probably be released with a slap on the wrist if caught. However, ecstasy, on the other hand, if I was caught selling, would put me back into double jeopardy of facing the rest of my life in prison.

I convinced myself that since it was less than 10 ecstasy pills that the customer was offering me, I could sell it within minutes, and that if caught, I could plead that it was for personal use.

As I had expected, the pills were sold within minutes. As I had also expected, the word got out that I was now selling ecstasy again. The calls and requests for ecstasy immediately came flooding in! I started doing the math in my head. I now had so many clients in my cell phone, more than I ever had in Bloomington or Florida. Plus, I now had contacts that had the funds to buy bulk amounts at a time. I thought carefully about it, and then made my decision. I was back to selling ecstasy!

I immediately called my client who offered me the ecstasy pills for my marijuana. I told him that I wanted to meet with the one he bought the ecstasy pills from immediately. He set up the meeting. We met, but his prices were much higher than I had been used to. Still, I bought some pills as a sign of good faith. Again, the ecstasy pills were sold within no time. Immediately, I began searching and asking other dealers in LA for the best prices for ecstasy.

I sit here now, 3 years later, in a one bedroom, luxury condominium in gorgeous Miami, Florida, shaking my head, just thinking of how crazy and reckless I used to be just a few years ago. It's a wonder that I am still alive. My journey here has certainly been incredible – simply amazing!

Flashback to Los Angeles, I called all my contacts around the country. This time, I was advertising to sell 10,000 to 100,000 ecstasy pills at a time! I had graduated to the majors! Although I never possessed those large amounts in my apartment, I had access to it!

For the following months, once again, I was a major drug lord! Between the ecstasy, marijuana, marijuana brownies that I baked and sold out almost daily, many, many customers were entering and exiting my humble apartment.

It was the same routine every day. They would come in and the artist, Young Jeezy would be blaring loudly in my CD stereo player. They would buy. I would usually up-sell. I would usually tell a few jokes. Then, they would leave a happy customer, with smiles on their faces. I loved all my customers. They always brought positive energy into my home.

Recalling those days makes me realize one of the reasons why I have been especially happy since living in Bloomington, Indiana. One reason is that I have almost always had a variety of positive energies coming into my home on a daily basis. I feed off of that energy. That positive energy is constantly being replenished.

Most people have thousands of friends and acquaintances in their lifetime, however when you think about it, only a select handful have the privilege and honor to come into your private world. That world is your home. I have been privileged to be able to say that thousands of amazing human beings have stepped foot into my private world, whether it was in the freshman dormitory in Indiana University, the many apartments that I resided in, over the course of the four years there, my brief stay in Florida, or my two apartments in Los Angeles, California. A large amount of awesome human beings have all shared a little piece of my world. That's what makes me connected to so many people. That is one reason I can relate to you. What I have given them, I have also received! That human connection is what brings pure bliss!

I was making so much money selling low and medium quality marijuana for months. My clientele list was climbing higher and higher. Then one day, I decided that I needed to control and limit the amount of clients that I was dealing with.

Something in my heart was telling me that I was dealing with too many people – that trouble may be near. It was the Spirit of God. I decided to start selling only high quality, high grade, elevated potency marijuana from then on. I was taking a huge risk in the business that I was running.

Usually, the lower the quality marijuana that you sell, the more clients that could afford to buy from you. The higher the quality, the more expensive marijuana that you sell, the less clientele that can afford it, and the less clientele that you have to sell to.

However, if you find the right customers who buy only high quality marijuana, then your profits could skyrocket and new doors would be opened as well. So, after careful consideration, I took the risk, because I knew that it was time for me to move on to a higher level if I was ever going to get out of the drug dealing business!

Almost overnight, my clientele base and profits dramatically transformed! I went from serving everyday average people, to serving extremely wealthy, affluent, and selective smokers. I was introduced to a whole new world of friends that, up until then, I had only dreamed of knowing.

Soon, I was being invited to dine in the finest restaurants, offered tickets to watch the NBA champion, Los Angeles Lakers play at the nearby stadium, invited to the most exclusive celebrity nightclubs, 5 star hotel pool parties, and given an endless amount of opportunities.

Before I knew it, I was one of the biggest drug dealers around! I would deal with the Triads gang on one transaction. I would deal with the Bloods and Cryps gang on other transactions. I would deal with pimps. I would deal with the Ethiopians. I would deal with the Nigerians. Other days, I would deal with the Mexican and Italian Mafia!

All these groups dealt with me for one reason – Trust! They knew that I would never work for the police and betray them. They could see in my eyes and hear the knowledge of my words, that I was only interested in one thing, the same thing that they were interested in – Money!

It seemed that we were all on the same fateful journey, just trying to make enough money as fast as possible to get out of the business. I was a shrewd business man. If the Mexicans overcharged me one day for drugs, then I would buy from the Triads. If the Triads overcharged on another day, then I would buy from the Italians…and so on.

I created a dynamic drug network. I depended on no one group or person. That gave me much power to demand the lowest prices. It had been about six years since I sold my first drug. I was now an expert. I was now a veteran! I felt as if I were living on a private island in my apartment complex. I was supplying virtually all my neighbors in my Mexican resort-like, luxury condominium complex.

Many days, you could see the aluminum foils that I wrapped my marijuana brownies with, as well as my signature baggies that I packaged the grams of marijuana in, littered around the condominium complex and even blocks away from the complex.

That's when I realized that I was getting bigger. Dealers who bought from me were giving me cars as collateral, in exchange for drugs. Not that I needed a car. By then, I had realized that it was best not to have a car at all. I was chauffeured everywhere by my limousine driver, or by wealthy friends in fancy cars, or I simply walked on foot to short distances.

I was buying drugs from my suppliers for such low wholesale prices, that one day, I realized that I did not have to buy in bulk any more. I could get a week or two supply of drugs for the same price as a multiple month supply. Now, if I were ever caught, I was secure that I would not serve much time in prison, if any at all. My suppliers were able to give me these deals, one, because they became great friends with me, and two, because they knew that I would always deliver! They knew that I would constantly sell out. They knew that I had charisma. They knew that I would always return with more and more money.

I was a drug cartel's dream, a constant marketer and salesman. They were always happy to get a call from me. It always meant that I was bringing money their way. I didn't give it much consideration back then, but my endless work ethic and money was feeding and providing for entire families around the country!

You could see the gratitude in their faces whenever a deal was completed. However, I was the one who was more grateful. I was getting closer and closer to my dream of getting out of dealing, and focusing on my athletic aspirations.

Then, before long, some of my high end clients began to request cocaine! Marijuana was bad. Ecstasy was worse. But cocaine, as always, in my mind, was on a completely different level! My logic for selling ecstasy and marijuana was that I had tried them both and felt that it wasn't too bad for the body when taken sparingly, in moderation.

I knew that cocaine, on the other hand, was very bad news, "the white devil" as they called it. If I thought that I was making a lot of money while selling ecstasy and marijuana, then I was making nothing, compared to when I started selling cocaine as well!

I was blind before, as to how many everyday people did cocaine. I was mind-blown to find out how many people did it. Almost everyone did it! My phone almost never stopped ringing. Some days, I would make a few thousand dollars. Customers would call me and be at my door at three, four, and five o'clock in the morning, sometimes as early as six in the morning! I was meeting so many beautiful women because of it.

When I first started dealing cocaine, I bought a few grams, and then I sold out immediately. Then, I bought an ounce, then immediately sold out once again. Next, I began buying quarter pounds of cocaine, selling out within days, sometimes hours!

Soon, I was looking to buy kilograms of cocaine! I was caught in a trance of becoming the biggest drug dealer by that time! Then one day, I had a sudden enlightenment.

I asked myself, "Maubrey, why do you want to buy a kilogram of cocaine, when you are getting ounces for the price that it would cost, if you divided the wholesale cost of a kilogram into ounces?!"

I did the math in my head. It was true. Somehow, I had managed to convince my cocaine suppliers to sell me ounces at extremely discounted prices. I was getting better at what I was doing!

After a few short weeks, just as I had done with the marijuana, I decided to sell only high quality, pure cocaine. The drastic positive feedback and frenzy by my clients was undeniable! My name instantly spread throughout Los Angeles as the man having the purest, finest cocaine. I wondered what the craze was about. Most of my clients had never had pure, uncut, Columbian cocaine in their lives.

Then the night came! No, not the night that I was arrested. The night that I decided to try cocaine! I had sworn to myself ever since I could remember, that I would never try cocaine! It was unthinkable in my mind. All my friends had done it, however I, on the other hand, would never even dream of it. But curiosity about what my clients were suddenly raving about, as well as temptation, overtook me. I reasoned to myself that after all, it was only a plant, and that I might as well try it once, while I am young, and since it was 100% pure, uncut cocaine.

I realize the foolishness of my rationalization as I write. Alone in my one bedroom condo that evening, foolishly, I inhaled a very small amount. I waited patiently for a few seconds. I had expected like the first time that I had smoked marijuana, to be taken to a different dimension. I had built up so much anticipation! I expected my mood and happiness to be elevated to peaks that I had never experienced before.

What did I feel...? I felt nothing special. I tried a larger amount. Again, I felt nothing special. Then, I got a sudden revelation from God that the "nothing special" feeling was exactly what the devil uses to trap man into using more, and more, and more, eventually becoming addicted, a slave!

I discontinued immediately! Within a few minutes that night, my stomach began to hurt as I gazed at the palm trees out of my third floor condo. My head ached. My body was rejecting the deadly, addictive plant. It was the Lord telling me that He did not want His son doing cocaine or any other harmful drugs.

I had to get myself together. I had two marijuana customers at my door. I told them that I had tried some cocaine. They asked me how it felt. With my eyes dilated, I told them. They sighed and shook their heads. They looked at me as if I were a fool. I could tell that they were disappointed in me. To them, I was different than the average drug dealer, and now, here I was, doing cocaine! They knew that I was smarter than that. I felt ashamed.

When they left, I called one of my best friends from New Jersey and told him that I had tried cocaine. He was surprised, yet nonjudgmental.

"I'm never doing this again… My stomach and head hurts. It's not worth it!" I said to him.

We spoke on the phone for some time longer, before saying good bye.

Since that evening, that was the first and last time I had ever foolishly tried cocaine. I'm always thankful to Christ for giving me supernatural will power to resist and reject many of the devil's temptations! Amen!

I've never told anyone else, besides my two customers that night, and my good friend from New Jersey, that I have tried cocaine, not even my older brother, and especially not my younger sister or parents!

Chapter 13

Day after wonderful, sunny California days went by. I was making descent money. I was becoming a highly efficient drug dealer. I became more watchful and careful not to fully trust anyone. I was meeting more and more clients by the day. My days consisted of waking up, making a few deals, working out, and relaxing at the pool and hot tub. I was in charge of my own empire. As always, I took calls and sold to clients at all hours of the night, whether it be 3, 4, or 5 in the morning. I worked hard, and I enjoyed life. Life around me was moving at the speed of light!

One week, I found out that one of my national clients that I had supplied to in the past was murdered in a drug related robbery. My heart hurt that day. A good and amazing human being was taken away!

Another week, my best friend, and former love, Stella told me that her boyfriend had proposed to her, and that she was getting married.

Just days later, one of my best friends called me, telling me that he was offered a job in Africa, and would be leaving the country within months.

It was a tough series of weeks for me. I felt that everyone close and dear to me was leaving me. Taylor was gone, my best friend, Stella was getting married, a friend was murdered, and another friend was leaving the country. I felt sad for some days. It was a somber time of reflection for me. I had to take a step back and reevaluate how I was spending my precious time in Los Angeles.

Finally, one day, I asked myself, "Why am I wasting my time thinking about just selling one kilogram of cocaine and tens of thousands of ecstasy?"

I saw myself in a much more magnified light! I decided to think bigger! I decided to be bold! I started asking all my various suppliers – the Italians, the Mexicans, the Bloods, the Cryps, the Triads, and the Africans, for 100 kilograms of cocaine, and 1,000,000 million ecstasy pills! I did not care anymore! I was more fearless of being killed or going to jail than ever before.

I knew that my direct suppliers themselves did not have that amount. However, I understood the concept that once I made the request, it would go up from middle man to middle man, all the way up to the source, who was probably a multi billionaire in a foreign country somewhere!

I was done with wasting time! I was ready to take the risk! My suppliers knew that I did not have the money to buy that amount, however they knew that if anyone could, I had the ability sell it all!

I get flashbacks and chills while writing to you. It is just amazing how daring and fearless I have been my entire life. After I sent out the bold requests, next, I started giving away my drugs on consignment – on credit. I knew that if I gave my drugs away on credit, that dealers would be more inclined to purchase from me. I would have a network of dealers selling for me, and I would have cash flowing in to me on a weekly and daily basis.

Then, as low prices as I was already getting my drugs for, I decided to search for new suppliers with even lower prices. As a Fortune 500 business would do, when trying to increase the bottom line, I was cost cutting. I was requesting absurdly low prices. But something in my head made me sure that those prices existed. People thought that I was crazy to ask for such low prices, however I knew exactly how much it cost to grow and manufacture the drugs, and with my experience and clientele, I was not willing to pay normal prices anymore.

Finally, after many weeks of persistently asking, and being directed to middle man after middle man, I was finally connected to a source that came the closest to the prices that I was demanding. But as fate would have it, it was too late!

In the previous months, I had loaned thousands of dollars worth of drugs and cash. I had become a bank. Some of my customers delayed in repaying my money. Some of my customers simply did not pay me back. Some claimed to have gotten the drugs that they were supposed to be selling for me stolen. Some customers used the drugs themselves. I remember thinking that it felt good to be secure, knowing that a majority of my neighbors and other clients owed me money.

However, the pace and size of cash flow had drastically decreased because of the risk that I had taken. I had gone back to my old reckless ways of managing my money, by reinvesting virtually every single dollar back into the business and not concerning myself with paying my fairly high monthly rent on time.

Once again, as in the past, I began to get eviction notices on my door. I ignored them. I would rather use my funds to buy in bulk and get cheaper prices for drugs, then pay my rent late, than to pay my rent on time and pay higher prices on bulk purchases simply because I was not spending as much cash. I thought that since I had been living in that apartment for almost a year now, that the management wouldn't evict me for being two months late.

Once again, I was wrong. Before I knew it, I was down to my last $4000 dollars in cash, and I was being evicted. I can't forget when the drug source that I had just been connected to came to my apartment. Just minutes before he arrived, I attempted to enter my apartment and realized that the apartment management had changed the locks. This was not good! I recall standing in the hallway, just outside my apartment door, attempting to calm my new source's nerves and extreme irritation that he was wasting time standing in open space with pounds of marijuana in his back pack.

He had never met me before. For all he knew, I could have been a police officer or someone who was going to rob him. I finally called one of my neighbors who I supplied to, and asked him to use his apartment to count the money and weigh the drugs.

Later in the day, I asked the apartment management to unlock my apartment door and to give me a day to move my possessions out and find a place to stay. They agreed.

Chapter 14

I wasn't ready to leave that paradise apartment complex just yet. The majority of my customers were my neighbors. I would be losing too much money had I went elsewhere.

So, I called all my neighbors who owed me money or did business with me in the past. I ended up living with a beautiful Italian woman in her late twenties, from New York, who happened to be a former exotic dancer! She kindly agreed to let me stay with her for a few weeks, until I found a place to stay. She was my angel. I will never forget her kindness! I struggle to know what I would have done, were it not for the kindness of her heart.

Needless to say, it was quite an interesting experience living with her. It seemed that all the men I knew, once they found out that I was living with her, wanted to pay me large sums of money to be able to sleep with her. The offers were very tempting to me, however, despite the fact that I was a drug dealer, I was definitely not willing to be a pimp. It was unthinkable. I loved her too much as a person to take money for her, even though it seemed that she would be willing to sleep with my client friends for money. I refused time and time again. I would stick only to what I was skilled at doing – selling drugs.

The daily amount of sales that I made dropped dramatically. Understandably, my new roommate was not comfortable with me inviting customers into her apartment as I had done in my place. I had to meet them downstairs in the hallway.

Needless to say, my clients did not like it. The sense of safety, coziness and comfort that I provided in my former apartment was gone. Little by little, I was losing all my clients. Looking back now, I can see what Christ was magnificently architecting in my life, the road He was leading me to…starting with the eviction, even though I could have easily paid my rent.

Weeks went by. By then, my angel of a woman offered to let me live with her, if I contributed to paying some of the bills. We drew close together, however, I had promised myself before hand, that I would not have sex with her, no matter what. I slept in the second bedroom, and she slept in hers.

After a few weeks of living with her, a 16 year old, Moroccan son of a friend of hers from New York, that she had told me would be moving in with her had arrived.

Now, I knew that I had to leave soon! A former exotic dancer, a drug dealer, and now, a 16 year old, minor child, living under the same roof!? I could feel trouble lurking in the air!

Weeks after he arrived, the boy and I began to bond. Typical of a 16 year old, he acted as if he were tough and thought he knew everything. But I could tell that he respected and admired the way that I carried myself. We would talk, and he would ask me an infinite amount of questions.

Some days, when there was no money, and the gas in the apartment was shut off because we did not pay, we would even make scrambled eggs in the microwave. It was quite comical during the meals.

We had no hot water for some time also, so I remember waking up early every morning, and walking to the apartment complex's gym just across from her apartment. I would work out and then use the gym shower.

We used to stay up many nights talking and laughing about how broke we were and how sad our situations were. I always had a sense of peace through those times though.

More and more, I was realizing how truly blessed by Christ I was! If I ever had any doubts, all I had to do was open my eyes, look around, and realize that I was living in a luxurious, two bedroom, two bathroom condominium, with a balcony overlooking a pool, waterfalls, hot tubs, and palm trees. If anything, my faith in Jesus was strengthening during those trying times.

The boy and I both had elaborate plans and big dreams for our futures. It wasn't before long, when he wanted to start selling marijuana like me. He felt that the money his parents were sending him from New York was far from sufficient.

I refused to sell marijuana or any other drug to him to resell. I could not live with it on my conscience to ever sell to a minor. I warned him of all the dangers every chance that I had. I told him to focus on school. I tried to bring out his gifts and interests.

During our many talks, he told me that he loved art. I then told him that instead of dealing drugs, he could create paintings and deal art.

"You're sixteen years old." I said to him, "You can create a painting and sell it to anyone if you just know how to explain and tell a story about it."

Those words that I spoke to him even inspired me.

"You know what?" I said to him, "If you finish this painting that you've started, and go out and buy a nice frame to put it in, I'll buy it from you for $100 dollars!"

It brings tears to my eyes as I write now. I could immediately see the bursting of ecstatic jubilation in his heart when I spoke those encouraging words to him. I cared so much for that stubborn 16 year old Moroccan boy that I had known for less than two months. I could see the dangerous path that he was headed.

Like me, he was overly ambitious, he knew that he could do anything in the world. Sometimes, I saw myself in him. I wanted to do anything to derail him from selling drugs and hanging around the crowd that he described he was with, during our many talks. I wanted to put money where my words were, so that he could always say honestly, that he sold his first painting for $100 dollars.

"Really?!" he exclaimed with wide open eyes.

"You're going to give me $100 dollars for this painting if I finish it and buy a frame!?"

"Yes." I responded.

"If you buy a nice frame, then I'll buy it from you for $100 dollars."

That afternoon, the 16 year old Moroccan boy finished the painting. The next day, he got a ride to the local shopping center and bought the cheapest wooden frame that he could find, framed his art, and presented it to me. I laughed in my head.

"I said a 'nice' frame." I thought to myself.

Nevertheless, not wanting to discourage him, I reached into my wallet and handed him a crisp $100 dollar bill.

"Wow...! Thanks Maubrey!" he exclaimed ecstatically, before giving me a big hug.

I struggle more to fight back the tears in my eyes now. I loved that kid. Tears now come running down the sides of my nose onto the corners of my lips, as well as down the sides of my cheeks.

Moments like those, are why life is worth living! To put a positive imprint in an innocent child's life, that will live on forever.

My heart sings a wonderfully happy song now, years after that day. I have bought much before and after that day, however, that simple, framed novice painting is certainly one of my most prized and inspiring purchases that I have ever made!

That painting symbolized hope! That painting symbolized love! I'm sure that where ever in the world that lost painting is now, it is in good hands.

However, as stubborn and hard headed as most teenagers are, within days, he found a way to start selling marijuana himself.

Now, I definitely had to get out of that apartment as soon as possible! Only if my parents back in New Jersey knew the environment that their bright son was in!

The Moroccan boy was saying drug names on the phone, mentioning the amounts and prices on the phone, saying our apartment address on the phone, instead of using code words, and making so many reckless choices and decisions in his dealings. I knew that it was only a matter of time until the police kicked in the door and sent us all to jail for a very long time. I could see the vision playing in my head over and over again.

And then if things weren't bad already, A few weeks after the 16 year old, now, drug dealing minor moved in, another exotic dancer, call-girl, flew in from New York to live with us.

Now there were four of us New Yorkers in one small, two bedroom condominium in Los Angeles, two exotic dancer women, and two African drug dealers, one of which was a 16 year old minor.

I could see the headlines in the front page of the Los Angeles Times newspaper if caught. I had to leave!

Meanwhile, my sales and customers were decreasing more and more every passing day. Soon, my angel wanted more money from me to pay for bills and expenses. Now, money that I would need to reinvest in buying drugs from my suppliers went to her.

Before I knew it, I suddenly found myself with less than a thousand dollars in cash and drugs. Still, she asked for more money, or I would have to leave and find another place to live.

It's amazing. I recall the 16 year old Moroccan boy, being worried for me daily after my angel told me that I might have to find another place to live.

"What are you going to do? Where are going to stay?" he used to ask me, aware that I would soon have to leave the apartment.

"Jesus will take care of me." I would answer. "He always does...!"

The boy marveled at my response. He was Muslim, and not Christian.

"How...? How...?" he would ask.

He could not comprehend how I could be so bold and confident, without worry, given the circumstances that lay ahead of me. He didn't understand how Christ had worked marvelous wonders in my life many times before.

I was fully convinced of The Lord's favor and love for me by then! I had no idea where my journey would lead me next, but I could feel in my heart that I was moving into a higher and greater dimension, as long as I did my part and believed steadfastly!

I did all that I could to stay. I raised and gave her hundreds of dollars within a matter of days, however, it was too little and too late.

In addition, there just was not enough room in the two bedroom apartment for all four of us. I held no resentment against her for driving me out. I knew that she loved me, but she had to make that hard decision. I love her and am eternally thankful for all that she did, for being a woman and inviting a stranger into her private world.

Those are the types of acts of kindness that stay forever ingrained in my memory. I bless her, where ever she is in the world today!

I thought long and hard about what I was going to do, and where I was going to go a few days before I had to leave the apartment. I decided that I still wanted to stay in that beautiful complex. I wasn't ready to leave just yet. I decided to call a few neighbors that I supplied marijuana to. They owed me about $1000 dollars combined. I imagined that they would not mind me living with them for some time. One of the two roommates that I had asked said he had no problem with me living with them, and that he just had to ask his roommate.

Chapter 15

Miraculously, the day that I had to leave the apartment, I received a call from him saying that I could stay with them! I was extremely relieved and humbled. I was amazed and glorified that once again, Jesus would allow two people, who were practically strangers, besides our drug transactions, to freely allow me to come into their private domain at last moments notice.

Granted, they owed me money, but know that they still could have refused to let me into their homes. If anything, the fact that they owed me money could have swayed them more, to not accept me into their home. I had been blessed yet again! They helped me move all of my possessions into their beautiful two bedroom, elevated ceiling, fourth floor loft.

It seemed that other friends of theirs had stored their furniture and other possessions at their condominium for the summer, so the place was packed with extra furniture in addition to possessions.

One roommate, Hunter, an art student from Kenya, slept in the loft upstairs, and the other roommate Dylan, also an Art student at the local art institution, slept on a futon in the living room, since his room on the main floor was congested with furniture. They gave me a sleeping bag, a pillow and some sheets, and I made my bed on the floor in a small corner of the congested main floor bedroom.

Understandably again, they too said that they would prefer that I don't bring my clients into the apartment. Once again, I had to call the few clients that I had left to inform them that I had relocated...again.

They could not have been excited about that. Although it was all in the same villa, I was now selling out of a third condominium within a few short months.

Living with my new friends, Hunter and Dylan, was one of the most enlightening experiences in my life. I must confess, although I had known them as my neighbors, for nearly one full year, they were not the type of friends that I could see myself with.

They were a few years younger than me, they were students, and their personalities, I gathered, were much different than mine. I imagine that they thought the same of me before I moved in with them.

But I can truly say that from the moment that I moved into their condominium, the learning process started, on both ends. My mind began to expand. My vision broadened. What I, personally learned from the experience was priceless!

I learned about art and design. I explored new and diverse ideas. We spoke about life many a night. We became wine connoisseurs. Every night, we would all pitch in a few dollars, and we would walk to the local mart and purchase a bottle or two of wine.

Those were one of my happiest times. I explored new sounds of music, from symphony to opera, to rap and rhythm and blues streaming through the condominium air each day. I learned new styles of culinary arts through them. I learned to share a little more, to give a little more. The three of us bonded as brothers. We seemed to understand and accept one another. I truly have nothing but fond memories of living with Hunter and Dylan.

Despite my newly discovered camaraderie, after a few weeks of living with them, I found myself with less than two ounces of marijuana, only a handful of customers, and less than a few hundred dollars to my name.

I had loaned so many people money. I had given away so much money. I had put my trust in so many people.

I had sold so much drugs. I had made so much money. But now, I was back to the freshman days in Indiana University, when I first started selling drugs with a few hundred dollars. I was back to square one! Everything had come back to full circle!

Was this my destiny? Was this where I was supposed to end up, after all those years?

Then one fateful day, I took a step back, and thought long and hard about the life that I was living, and about my future.

That day, finally, after nearly six long years of dealing drugs, I decided that after I was finished selling my last few ounces of marijuana, I would no longer sell drugs again! That was it! The Angels in Heaven rejoiced! My heavenly Father rejoiced! Finally, His son had gained wisdom!

All the signs were ever too clear. The Lord Jesus had masterfully architected the series of events, shielding me from danger, in the process to lead me to that divine enlightenment.

As if the sound of thunder and lightning had exploded in the sky, the devil had awakened! The devil sprung to action! Just days after I had made my life changing decision that I would soon quit selling drugs, I received an ecstatic call from one of my major suppliers, that she had been trying to reach me for days! She told me that the supplier with the million ecstasy tablets that I had requested had arrived into the country!

A million ecstasy tablets! I can just picture the sight of it.

"Oh, no..." I said to her on the phone, shaking my head, with a smile on my face.

"I'm not in the business anymore."

I had been pestering her, non-stop, for months to see if the supplier was back in the country, but to no avail. Now, just days after making my mind up to stop selling drugs, here came the phone call that I had been waiting so long for.

I could easily have changed my mind, and went to meet her. With my national network of dealers and clients that I had established throughout the years, I could easily have sold one million tablets within days!

This was the break that I had been waiting so long for! Still, my mind was set. I was through with living an illegal, sinful life! The day that I had been waiting for ever since the day I began selling drugs had arrived, yet I turned it down for the sake of good. I turned it down for the sake of Jesus!

We spoke a bit longer before ending the call. I never heard back from that wonderful, beautiful Asian woman again. I will always keep her in my prayers for what she did for me, and how kind she treated me, as if I were part of her family. I pray that she too has found harmony, happiness, and balance through Christ! She truly was a good spirit.

I had passed the test! The heavens rejoiced once more!

But the devil was not done yet! Just another few days later, as I was walking through my condominium complex, a neighbor of mine, who I had also asked months before, if he knew of anyone who had 100 kilograms of cocaine, stopped me, extremely ecstatic as well. He told me that he finally found a contact that was willing to give me 100 kilograms of cocaine, millions of dollars worth, on consignment! Again, I laughed and shook my head.

"I'm out of the business, man..."

He seemed shocked! This wasn't the ambitiously reckless Maubrey that he had come to know. Again, I could have easily made a few calls, sold the 100 kilograms of cocaine and become a multi-millionaire, literally, overnight! But still, my mind had been set! I would finish selling the last few grams of marijuana and I would be done! Done for good!

Over the course of the following days, I received many lucrative drug offers from the Italians, the Cryps, the Bloods, and many others. I turned them all down!

Isn't it interesting how the devil works the hardest to keep man trapped in the web of sin?

I knew that I did not want to be a drug dealer anymore. I knew that I still wanted to follow my dreams. I had no idea how it was going to happen now that I wasn't making large amounts of money.

Should I heed the advice of my parents and siblings, and return home to New Jersey? Should I get a normal job? Should I keep looking for opportunities?

Strangely, I was at peace, however, I was lost. I felt all alone in a state with no family or long time friends. I stood there that sunny afternoon, alone in the quiet, cluttered room that I slept in.

Then suddenly, I looked down at my opened suitcase.

And there it was! The Holy Bible!

Years before, my mother had packed that small hand sized Bible in my luggage during one of my visits back home. Every once in a while I would notice it, however, I was never inclined to open it.

Now, alone in the room, it was clear as day that it held all the answers to all my deepest questions. It seemed as if the sun's rays shinned a bright beam of light directly onto the holy book! It was a true moment of revelation for me!

Months before, I suddenly had a burning desire to be the wisest, smartest person alive, and had been praying on it ever since. I wanted to be a pure and whole man. I wanted to have the answers to all problems and adversities.

As I stared at the Bible, as if it were a treasure chest, which it was indeed, I decided that I was going to do what many men, for centuries, have failed to do! I was going to read the entire bible, Old and New Testament, word for word, chronologically, from beginning to end, from the book of Genesis to the book of Revelation!

Friend, I can testify to you that the moment I made that decision, I could feel in my entire body that the wheels of time had paused momentarily, and had shifted to my favor!

The windows of Heaven opened for me. I was transformed into a new man! I was transported into a new world, an elevated dimension of life! On that fateful, glorious afternoon, my new life began!

I recall going to a small church in Bloomington, Indiana, one summer, during the time that I was living in the homeless shelter, and unsuccessfully attempting to read the Bible from the first page. I read a few pages in the book of Genesis, and then stopped because I felt that it was too difficult to focus on, and comprehend the grammar.

Perhaps, it wasn't yet my time. This time, a few years later, my mind was ready!

Before I started reading the Bible, I imagined it being a book with thousands of pages of tedious laws and rules that we had to follow.

As I began to read page after page, I quickly came to the realization that it is a book of great stories of mankind, human interactions, sins, and true love, just as in a bestselling novel written today.

I was enlightened! I was amazed! I was inspired! My excitement grew daily, as I shared some of the stories with my new roommates. I immediately began to view life in an entirely new manner. I felt a sense of peace and well being that I had never experienced before. I knew that all would be well. Words cannot begin to describe the way my world and the people in it suddenly changed for the better.

One simple, yet wonderful memory that stands out to this day, was when Hunter and Dylan invited me to join them at a house gathering at one of our neighbor's apartments on the opposite end of the complex. I recall drinking a beer while learning to play chess for the first time in my life.

Later in the evening, a slightly chubby, but beautiful girl, around the same age as us, walked into the apartment with some other friends. She had long golden locks. Her face seemed to be glowing. She was joyful and happy that she had bought some antique items from a garage sale in Beverly Hills.

For some reason, she gravitated to me fairly quickly. She was holding a freshly cut red rose in her hand.

"Smell it." she said to me with a blissful smile on her face after inhaling a deep whiff of the red rose through her nose.

"Ok, sure..." I said, a bit puzzled as to what the big deal was.

I had seen and smelled roses a number of times growing up. From the instant the aroma of that lusciously fragrant red rose entered my nostrils, an explosion of endorphins went off in my entire body! I was in love! It was pure euphoria! I had been taken to cloud nine!

Never in my life had I experienced such an aroma! Tears almost rolled out of my eyes. My heart was filled with such joy! At that moment, I knew that the Lord had sent this angel to me to deliver me a message – a message that there were more magnificent hidden treasures and discoveries to come as a result of my obedience to Him!

I thought of how many other secret treasures of goodness that was out there, that my many sins had blinded me from seeing, receiving and experiencing.

My enlightenment process continued. The girl and I conversed for some time afterwards. She spoke of how her dream was to be in television commercials.

"Wow!" I thought to myself, "How simple and humble."

She did not want to be a big time actress like the majority of people in Los Angeles. She just wanted to act in commercials. I was amazed! What a humble concept. I encouraged her.

I too shared my dreams of becoming the greatest athlete and model. As we continued speaking, she told me that she had been a ballroom dancer for the majority of her life. Upon my request, she even agreed to demonstrate her gift right there in the apartment, as she explained to me what she was doing.

I was amazed evermore! I felt as if I were in a wonderful dream. I had seen ballroom dancers in movies and on television a few times in my life and thought nothing of it. But I had never been privileged to see a demonstration in person.

Christ was surely showering me with abundant goodness that evening. It was not long before I took a moment to digest the fact that I was surrounded in an apartment full of wonderful human beings. These were the kind of friends that I needed in my life. Blessed indeed was I! They had no idea, but being with them, that evening changed my life. Great friends are the true treasures that we are unknowingly seeking in life!

The blessings did not stop that evening. A few days later, out of the blue, I received a message online, from an internationally well noted artist and photographer, requesting me to meet and work with him.

We met many times in his office. We would talk for hours. Little did I know that he was preparing me for the promises that lay ahead. He told me how beautiful a man he thought I was. He further strengthened my confidence in myself. I knew that he loved me.

Chapter 16

Days later, as I sat waiting in the LAX airport terminal, on my way to watch my younger sister graduate from high school, I received a somewhat hysterical phone call from him, grieved that I was leaving without notice.

"I'll be back from New Jersey in a few days." I said, attempting to calm him down.

Up until then, I had no idea the effect that I had on people. I certainly was oblivious that I had such an effect on men. I realized that with great power, comes great responsibility and compassion.

He revealed to me that he had spent the past 24 hours, with hardly any sleep, painting a portrait of me. My mind was blown! I was humbled and honored that an internationally known artist would spend his valuable time painting a portrait of me.

I was beginning to see who I was, and what I was to the world!

After returning from New Jersey, days later, he allowed me into his beautiful home and art gallery in Beverly Hills to unveil the painting to me.

Days before, he had been warning me that I was not prepared to see the painting. He said that I would shed many tears after seeing it. I, on the other hand, could not imagine a mere painting that would bring me to tears. I thought it was impossible. I dismissed his warnings.

Lo and behold, when he finally unveiled the portrait painting of me, and left me alone in the hallway for a moment, I stared at the portrait for a few seconds.

Suddenly, my deepest hidden emotions raced, like a tidal wave to my head. And out came bursting a sea of tears from my eyes. I cried aloud, trying my best to hold it in.

From our hours of conversations in such a short time period, the man had figured out the core of who I truly was, and had managed to portray it in a single painting.

Passionate! Uncertain! Driven! Loving! Continuously searching! Eternally believing! Ambitious! Sad! Lonely! Vulnerable!

That one portrait exuded all those adjectives of me. Ah, as I write now, with the image of that painting in my head, how the emotions and butterflies return to my body.

"African Man", the title of the painting was – true indeed!

He came in the hallway as I wept, and hugged me as a father would hug a son. I cried on his shoulder for a moment longer, as he comforted me, telling me that it would be ok.

I was transformed yet again that afternoon! I knew that, yes, everything was going to be ok. Yes! All my dreams would come true! Yes! All my ambitious goals would come to fruition!

I had much more to learn on my symphonic journey ahead! Meeting David Harris allowed me to further know and understand who I was. It allowed me to be more open to the world – to communicate my feelings – to break out of my metaphorical shell. I will always thank God for putting him on my path!

Meanwhile, I was down to my last few measures of marijuana to sell. I had a few hundred dollars to my name. Friends and clients still owed me thousands of dollars. Other new roommates had moved in with us to help with the rent. Hunter had moved from the apartment and out of California.

By then, I had been living with them for about a month. When Hunter left, and the new roommates moved in, Dylan told me that I would need to find another place to live. The apartment had become too crowded for us all. I had nowhere in mind to go, however, I understood.

It was time for me to continue in my journey forward. Dylan suggested that I either move back home with my parents, or that I ask Christopher, another neighbor who owed me money, to stay with him for some time.

My parents had been planning a two week vacation back to Africa that August to celebrate one of my aunts' 60th birthday. My parents, my aunts, and a few cousins were all planning on flying to Ghana from London to be there. I would also get to meet my grandparents, my half brothers and sisters, as well as other family members, who I had not seen since being swept away from Ghana about 20 years before.

My parents had been asking me to join them for months now. At that point, my decision was to stay with Christopher for a few weeks, and then return home to New Jersey for a few days before traveling to Ghana for two weeks.

I'll never forget Christopher's answer after I nervously asked him if I could stay with him for a few weeks in his one bedroom apartment. I was sure he would give me a reason why it would not be a good idea.

Christopher and I had been at odds for a few months earlier that year. He owed me money, as many people who surrounded me did, and he always gave me a reason why he could not pay me back.

I had also heard through another customer that he would tell potential clients not to buy marijuana from me, and that he would insult me.

"Absolutely!" he exclaimed without hesitation.
"Do you need me to help you move your stuff in?"
I stood there surprised and dumbfounded on the opposite end of the call.

"Umm… Yeah, that would be awesome! Thank you so much, Christopher!" I replied.

After hanging up the phone, I looked to the heavens and thanked the Lord for Christopher. I was truly humbled at that hour. Never in my life had I seen anyone, without hesitation welcome a stranger or even a good friend into their home. My blessings were continuing!

Chapter 17

My plan, after returning from Ghana, was to fly back to Los Angeles and move into an apartment in the town of my dreams since I was a child –Beverly Hills!

Once again, I had no idea how I would do so, but as you have witnessed, I was able to move into president's quarters and "The Boulders" in Bloomington, Indiana, after living in a homeless shelter for a month. I was able to move into "The Villa Azure" a year after setting my mind and believing.

By that point in my life, there were no limits, no boundaries, and no doubts as to what I was capable of achieving through Christ!

But this time around, I would achieve seemingly impossible feats the good way, the legal way, the Godly way!

The wisdom that I was obtaining from my readings of the Bible was assuring me that the only direction that I would be going onward was up! I believed that wholeheartedly!

Words cannot explain how happy and excited I was, once I had made the decision to return back to Africa! I must have told every neighbor that I ran into during my final weeks in Los Angeles. I could see their eyes brighten, and their smiles widen, as they shared in my joy.

I needed a break from America. I needed to return to my roots. I needed to further expand my mind. A few days later, Dylan and another neighbor helped me move all my possessions, with the exception of two suitcases of clothes, into a storage building a few blocks away.

I still remember the storage company's advertisement now. "Only $1 for the first month of storage!"

I laugh now, knowing the outcome of my decision to store all of my possessions with them. I paid the dollar and then was off to my neighbor, Christopher's condominium.

I must say, it was quite interesting living with Christopher. He was a very unique human being. Our personalities connected quickly. I quickly learned that I was living with someone that was as strange and as different as I was.

Instantly, all animosity between us in the past was forgiven and forgotten. It wasn't before long, that I realized why he was the way he was.

Throughout the year that I had known him, many of our neighbors and mutual friends would say that he was just a spoiled, rich kid, who lived off of his parents' money.

Others called him lazy. Others called him a user and a taker. To be quite honest, that had been my impression of him throughout the year of knowing him, especially since he had owed me hundreds of dollars.

However, living with Christopher after just a few days made me realize something remarkable. Christopher's way of thought was quite possibly of the purest form. The reason he was so carefree in his asking and taking was because he was so carefree in his giving and helping others. It was such a revelation to me!

I looked back at all the times in the past that mutual friends and neighbors would be dumbfounded and sometimes insulted and offended about his freeloading character. He didn't seem to comprehend the value of money.

Now, it all made sense. I thanked God for giving me a forgiving and humble heart, to ask Christopher to live with him, despite our past disputes.,

Had it not been for forgiveness and humility, I would not have learned this very valuable life's lesson!

Christopher was a good man. Although he was surrounded by nice and luxurious things, he put no high value on any of them. Within a second, he could part with a valuable possession of his. I was learning evermore and absorbing all the positive lessons that I was learning through him.

I began to know the reason why the Lord had brought me to Christopher. Unbeknownst to him, I was sent there to continue my education. My daily routine stayed the same, this time, with the awareness that I would be leaving Los Angeles in a few weeks, with the unspoken, but hovering possibility of not returning.

I slept in the corner of the living room floor of Christopher's one bedroom apartment. I awoke to the pages of the Bible and a prayer early each morning. I felt so safe and protected by Jesus. I would then put on my workout clothes and leave the apartment for my morning workout.

During my runs, I always marveled at the absolutely gorgeous parts of my neighborhood that were just blocks away, that I had never explored, and had no idea existed the entire year that I had been living in the area.

Upon my return from running, I would always knock on Christopher's locked room door for long periods of time, attempting to wake him up and open the door so that I could brush my teeth and shower in the bathroom.

"It's too early..." he would always mumble, half asleep.

I would laugh and continue to bang the door some more until he got out of bed and opened the door.

Before I arrived, he was not accustomed to starting his day before noon. During the day, we would go our separate ways, taking care of what we had to do on our schedules.

Our friendship seemed to magnify each passing day. We shared the little resources that we had. We became brothers. When he didn't have, one day, I would give. When I didn't have, one day, he would give.

Knowing that I had a specific healthy diet, one week, when I did not have money, he invited me to go grocery shopping with him. I can still recall him filling the shopping cart with an abundance of food, which he paid for.

It is those kinds of little gestures of kindness that matters most to me. Every once in a while, I would give him a small amount of the now little marijuana that I had remaining.

Another day, he would treat me to dinner at an Italian restaurant. My brother, Christopher had become. We were working as a team. Before long, he suggested that we rent a two bedroom apartment and become roommates upon my return from Africa.

Now, more than ever, I was realizing the effect that I had on people as I kept my heart pure. Many a day, we spent telling jokes, laughing, having women over the apartment, drinking wine, and talking about our goals and dreams for the future.

As I did with my buddies, Dylan and Hunter, I had managed to turn Christopher into a wine connoisseur too. Ah, what great memories!

He dreamt big, just like me. He also shared with me a few adversities that he was going through. I encouraged him that if he just goes through the process with a believing and confident heart, and simply keeps being a good person, then all would work out for his best. I could tell that he valued my advice.

The divine connection that the Lord Jesus had created between us was wonderfully uncommon! I had found a lifetime friend, once again, at the most unexpected place.

It really hit me one day, after my running workout, like a bolt of lightening, where in the country I was living, and how truly blessed I was to be in such a paradise city! It took me two whole years, and the possibility of leaving for good, to reach that epiphany.

Finally, the day had come! After selling hundreds and hundreds of thousands of drugs, I sold my last gram of marijuana and was done! I was out of the illegal drug business for good! Amen and Hallelujah! The heavens rejoiced and celebrated! The angels began to sing in jubilation! The trumpets sounded! The transformation continued!

I recall Christopher giving me a nice, brand new, white, button down, collared shirt as a gift the day before I left Los Angeles. He told me that it was an old shirt of his, but I could tell that he had just gone out and bought the shirt for me. What a guy! A big smile came across my face. My heart was joyous. I hadn't expected anything from Christopher. He had given and helped me more than I could have ever imagined.

"Thanks, brother!" I said to him in gratitude.

I continued to smile. At that moment, I was sure that he loved me as his brother. He was too modest and embarrassed to tell me that he had went out and bought me a brand new shirt.

I enjoyed my final full day in L.A. We toasted our last glass of wine. I packed my luggage during the late hours of the night as I reminisced about two of the most amazing and adventurous years that I had ever had in my life in Los Angeles.

I thought about all the good times that I had. I thought about all the life lessons that I had learned. I thought about all the great, lifetime friends that I had made. I thought about all the angels, in "The City of Angels", that Jesus Christ had sent my way – like the time that Taylor and I were late on our rent, and we were getting eviction warnings from the apartment management. We struggled for weeks to find help, when miraculously, a friend, Cameron Martin, agreed to loan me over $2000 dollars in cash.

"I can help you brother. Can you find a way to get to my apartment?" he asked me on the phone.

My heart skipped a beat. I pumped my fist and praised the Lord after getting off the phone with Cameron. That day, I can honestly say, was one of the most moving and inspirational days of my life! It forever changed my life. It changed the way I thought. It boosted my faith in Christ! No one in my life had ever loaned me $2,000 dollars. That type of generosity was inconceivable to me at the time.

I recall taking a taxi about an hour away to his home, one night, thinking and marveling about how truly blessed I was through Christ. When I got to his apartment building, Cameron came downstairs, extremely exhausted from a long day of traveling, with a thick white envelope filled with $2,000 dollars in cash. I thanked him dearly, gave him a big hug, and got back into the cab.

When I returned home to my princess, Taylor, and showed her the money. She was absolutely shocked! She marveled in awe! We were truly blessed! I was able to pay Cameron back the money that he had borrowed me, just a few weeks later.

As I continued to pack my clothes for my exodus from Los Angeles, I thought about another great measure of favor, mercy, and blessing that the Lord had poured onto me.

Late one night, I was in a dance club. I was standing by the bar, inconspicuously selling herbal ecstasy pills to customers who passed by me. I was dressed extremely sharp, wearing black, loafer shoes, fitted jeans, a collard, buttoned, solid black shirt under an all white blazer jacket. I had on diamond studded earrings in both of my earlobes, a freshly shaved bald head, and a diamond bezel watch. I was radiating that night!

A man named Isaac approached me, complimented me and began to converse with me. He soon introduced me to a few of his friends in the nightclub who wanted to buy ecstasy from me. We walked around the huge, packed nightclub and talked about our bigger than life dreams about the future.

By the end of the night, he had helped me sellout my entire supply of ecstasy pills. We exchanged contact information, and I exited the club with about $1,000 in cash in my pocket.

Over the course of the following weeks, we kept in touch. He introduced me to many of his friends who became clients of mine.

Then one day, Isaac called me, telling me that he wanted to introduce me to some friends from out of town.

"Can you drive down to Santa Monica Beach?" he asked.

"I don't know" I said, "I'm waiting on a call from a few big clients."

"Well," I recall him replying, "Let me be a 'big client'."

I laughed.

"Ok, I'll come, and I'll bring enough." referring to the pills.

Excited but cautious as always, I got into my black BMW and made my way to a beautiful, luxury hotel on Santa Monica Beach. I entered the hotel's magnificent lobby, and strolled around, as I waited patiently for Isaac and his friend to arrive.

I laugh now. I'll never forget the feeling in my stomach when I saw Isaac walk up with his friend, John. My heart pounded like a fast paced, base drum. John, in his swim trunks after getting out of the hotel's pool, was a massive 6' foot tall, 200 plus pound, muscular man in his mid 40's. His muscles were bulging and well defined.

The very first thing I thought as we walked toward one another to shake hands in the lobby of that beach front hotel, was that, this man has got to be DEA - a Drug Enforcement Agent, or with the FBI - the Federal Bureau of Investigation!

I thought, for sure, that my time had come! I thought, for sure that, that was the day that I would be sent away to jail for a very long time!

"Oh, boy," I thought to myself, "I'm in the 'big leagues' now! How did I get myself into this situation?"

Still, I moved forward, kept a composed face, smiled, and shook Isaac and John's hand. I threw out my fear. I reminded myself that if he was indeed a federal officer, then they would soon be surprised that the pills were not illegal (so I thought at the time).

We went to meet his other friends outside at the hotel's lavish pool area. After talking and lounging for sometime by the pool, John, Isaac, and I proceeded up to their hotel room. I sold John over a dozen tablets, exchanged contact information, shook hands, and then Isaac walked me to the front of the hotel.

I thanked Isaac for yet another connection. We shook hands, and then parted ways. I was back in my BMW and cruised my way home.

My entire drive home, I recall being incredibly nervous, imagining that, at any moment, at any stop light, a team of federal swat cars would come out of the blue and surround my black BMW.

Even after arriving back to my condominium, I was preparing for my door to be kicked in by federal agents. It just felt too easy of a drug transaction – the luxury, beach front Santa Monica hotel, the fast easy money, the muscular buyers, and beautiful woman that John's friend was with by the hotel pool, their friendly, amazing personalities… Everything just felt too good to be true.

Well, I had no reason to worry. No agents kicked in my door that day. Isaac and John met me at a nightclub on Sunset Boulevard later that evening. Isaac ended up leaving early, so John and I stayed, talked, and danced with women for the remainder of the evening. At the end of a good night, we said goodbye, parted ways, and that was the last I saw of John.

However, the story does not end there. A few months later, after Taylor had left me, once again, I had delayed paying my rent for months, and instead, invested my money in pounds of marijuana and tablets, in order to get the cheapest prices.

The management had sent me a notice that if I did not pay the over $5,000 dollars in rent that I owed them within a few days, then I would be evicted. I panicked! At that time, I had tens of thousands of dollars in drugs, but there was no way that I could sell $5,000 worth of drugs within a few days without taking a huge loss in profits.

I decided to call all the friends and clients who I had loaned money to in the past. For hours and for days, I stayed on the phone calling numerous people to repay me or loan me the money.

One by one, people gave me reasons why they could not help. Some suggested that I get evicted and move to a cheaper apartment. I was not willing to concede! It was not yet my time to leave.

I remember looking through all the business cards that I had collected over the year. I called many. Still, no one was willing or able to help.

Finally, I came to the business card that John had given me in the hotel room, the day we first met. I recall admiring his business card more than any of the other hundreds of business cards that I had collected. It was a black, sturdy, plastic card with his contact information on it. It reminded me of the American Express Black Card that has an unlimited credit line. To me, it signified infinite wealth and abundance.

I felt bad to call him, being that I had only met him for less than two or three hours of my life. Who would give a boy $5,000 dollars after only meeting him for a few hours? He had flown back home to Myrtle Beach, South Carolina, the complete opposite end of the country! Why would he risk giving virtually, a complete stranger $5,000 dollars, and risk never seeing me or his money again?

But the Lord told me to reach out and connect with John. I had nothing to lose. I had run out of options. He was my last hope. I said a brief prayer to Jesus, and then picked up my cell phone and began to dial.

To my surprise he answered. I asked him if he could help me, and then spoke for much time explaining my emergency. I assured John that I would pay him back as I received money.

And then, there was silence. I will never forget what John said to me as he began to speak.

"Maubrey, thank you for considering me a friend, to be able to call me, and ask for my help. I'm honored..." he continued.

"I'm not a rich man, you know... I have children and family to take care of. I just had a newborn baby, but I will give you the $5,000 to pay your rent. The money is not mine, Maubrey. But it is for the Lord, Jesus."

My heart raced! My mind was boggled by the words that I was hearing!

He asked, "Maubrey, are you a believer?" referring to whether I believed in Jesus Christ, the Son of God.

"Yes. I am." I answered with certainty and humility.

"This money does not come from me, Maubrey, but from Him. You can repay me as you receive the money. And even if you are unable to pay me back, I don't care..."

Wow...!

I almost shed tears as I listened on the phone. I had never heard these words about such a large amount of money in my life! I was convinced, once again, that the majesty of Jesus was on my side! He had entered John's heart, and given him the compassion to give cheerfully and effortlessly!

Before getting off the phone, John led in a prayer to Christ, of thanks, hope, and encouragement.

When I got off the phone with John, I felt empowered! I felt enlightened! I felt humbled! Everything I thought about money, giving, helping, and worldly possessions was forever changed! My life was never the same again! With a single breath from Jesus into my direction, with a snap of a finger, and a blink of an eye, I had just witnessed a miracle!

It's amazing how you receive a miracle when you most need it. As a child growing up, the Lord had given me dreams and visions of meeting people such as John. John even physically resembled the ones in my visions.

I was realizing that those divine dreams and visions as a child were becoming my reality, more and more, each passing day, during the purification and cleansing of my heart!

Just a few days later, even to the surprise of the friendly apartment management women, John called the office, and wired about $5,000 dollars just in time! I had found a brother in Christ! I had found a mentor! I had found a lifetime friend! Amen! Hallelujah!

To this day, more than three long years later, as I sit here writing in beautiful Miami, Florida, John is one of, if not, the dearest companion that I have. I always thank the Lord Jesus for that divine connection, that fateful day in the hotel lobby!

Late that evening, on the eve of my Los Angeles exodus, I packed the last article of clothing into my suitcase. At approximately 4 A.M. in the morning, I knocked on my brother, Christopher's door.

"It's time!" I said to him, waking him from his deep sleep.

"Ughh..." he groaned.

I smile now. He was by no means used to waking up anywhere near that time of the day. He dragged himself out of bed and opened his room door. I smiled. This was the end of another wonderful chapter in my life. We spoke for some time about Africa and about plans for when I returned to The States.

"Bring me back a gift." he said with a smile.

"No problem." I replied.

Minutes later, my taxi cab had arrived. It was time! Christopher helped me take my luggage to the taxi cab. For the final time, I embraced the magnificent beauty of the condominium complex that I had called home for more than a year. I watched as the morning dew ascended from the lush, green grass, and marveled as vapor rose from the pool.

It was such a surreal and marvelous sight. The peace and calm in the air that was, that morning the Lord had created, I could cry a teardrop. This was it!

I thanked Christopher for all he had done for me. I wished him nothing but the best for his future. We hugged and said good bye. I was in the taxi, off to Los Angeles Airport.

It is amazing, the kind of human bond that Christ can form in such a short amount of time. I had given a seed of love and kindness to Christopher in the past. In return, the King had yielded a harvest of divine friendship, far into the future!

Chapter 18

PRODIGAL SON

Hours later, I was amongst the clouds, en route to my past…en route to my future! Good bye Los Angeles, my Heaven on Earth! Good bye "City of Angels"! Christ had sent His Angels to my rescue, without fail, each time I cried His name!

With the Holy Bible at my side, I arrived in "The Garden State", New Jersey, a new and wiser man. With the exception of a few brief visits from time to time, I had been away from home and away from my family for over six whole years!

I left home at the age of 17 years old, as a wide-eyed, inexperienced boy, full of belief, hope, and promise. I had been through so much. I had conquered many mountains. I had been in the lowest valleys. I had explored the country. I had made many poor choices. I had amassed abundant wealth. I had lost it all. I had gained true wisdom, knowledge, and priceless, unforgettable life experiences.

And now, the prodigal son was back! My family warmly embraced me upon my return. We celebrated and feasted. I could tell that they were jubilant to have me back, close to them, where they could watch, advise and protect me.

None of my family, except my older brother had any idea, what kind of illegal life I had been living in Los Angeles. Perhaps, they suspected. But nothing mattered now. I was back home! They missed me dearly. I too, missed them dearly.

In Los Angeles, I envisioned coming to live with my family, as I had done growing up as child, one last time, before I fully became a man and started a family of my own. Being away from home for so many years made me realize how short life really was. I knew that I may never get a chance to spend countless hours, days, and months with my family, as I had during my wonderful childhood.

This could be my final opportunity for my vision to turn into a reality. Only the Lord would decide. However, my mind was still set on returning to Los Angeles shortly after returning to New Jersey from Africa.

Within a few weeks after returning to "The Garden State", my mother's, my father's, and my luggage was packed. My younger sister was preparing for her first year in university, and my older brother was in Spain, on vacation. My parents and I were on our way to the airport for our homeland in Africa – Ghana!

However, the journey would not come without stumbling blocks and adversities. When we arrived to check-in our luggage at the airport, we were told that I could not board the plane because I needed additional documents from the Ghanaian Embassy. My heart dropped!

A thought immediately went through my head that it may have something to do with me formerly being a drug dealer. I had built up so much anticipation to travel to Ghana, and now, there was a possibility that I would not be going.

We decided that my mom should travel to Ghana ahead of us, and that my dad and I would go to the embassy first thing in the morning for the required additional documents.

I can't forget the fond feeling that I had en route to the Ghanaian Embassy, early the next morning in New York City. For the first time in a very long time, I felt a magnified father-son bond with my dad, as we walked miles through the New York City streets.

Our journey was long. We were on a mission! We were on a mission to get me to Ghana!

Even when we arrived at the embassy, there was hesitation and a delay in processing my paperwork. They were not sure whether the person in my passport and green card photos was me. I was about 6 years old in my passport photo, and about 13 years old in my green card photo.

My face, my bone structure, and my skin tone had drastically changed so much over the years, that a supervisor had to come to the window to confirm my identity.

I pressed forward optimistically! There was nothing that would stop me from going to Ghana! We got the documents and then we journeyed through the big city and the trains back home.

Once again, very early, the following morning, my dad and I were on our way to the airport. There was still a possibility that I would have to wait a few days before going to Ghana.

"Don't worry. You will get on the plane today." my dad said confidently.

When we got to the airport attendant to present all our documents, I noticed that there was still that big exclamation mark, red flag on his computer screen, that the previous attendant had entered the day before, to show that I was not supposed to travel.

My heart raced as I kept a composed face. Within seconds after presenting our documents to the attendant, he smiled and handed my dad and me our tickets. I exhaled a huge sigh of relief! It was almost as if the Lord prevented the attendant from seeing the enormous, red exclamation mark on the computer screen. I was meant to go to Africa!

The Lord showed me that He was still working for my good! My heart raced, as my dad and I sat on the plane awaiting take off. I could not believe that after over 20 years, it was finally happening! I was returning to Ghana!

Moments later, we were miles high, me, crossing the Atlantic Ocean for my first time as an adult, on our way to a connecting flight in the Netherlands. The heavenly images of the blue ocean, the white clouds, and the blue sky, as we floated in the air will always remain with me!

I dozed off eventually. Later, I opened my eyes to the sound of the captain informing us that we would be landing in the Netherlands shortly. My eyes were amazed yet again! I had never witnessed such beautiful, lush landscapes before! The hills, the mountains, the clouds, the sky – what had I done to deserve such a treasure for my senses?

I was in a whole new world! My mind expanded evermore! I can still smell the aroma of the absolutely fresh Netherlands air when we landed. The endorphins in my entire body ran wild! I had never been pleasured with such an aroma in my life! My heart melted with each breath that I took.

"Is this only the beginning of what You have promised me, as long as I followed Your ways?" I asked Jesus.

The answer was a strong "Yes! This is only the beginning!"

Even the women who worked in the airport, with their powder blue and white, futuristic uniforms seemed surreal. They all smiled at me and seemed so friendly. I had found another Heaven on Earth! I could have lived in that airport and be a happy man.

The secret is traveling, my friend... The secret is traveling!

My dad just smiled the entire time, aware of what my mind was experiencing. I was truly humbled that afternoon. I could almost hear what my dad was thinking.

"All these years, son... You thought you knew everything about the world. You thought you knew more than me. Well, this should show you that I am still your loving father. I have been to, and been through much more places than you could ever imagine."

In a sense, that was what my Heavenly Father was also telling me.

"All these years, son... You thought you knew everything about the world. You thought you knew more than Me. Well, this should show you that I am still your loving Father. I have been to, and been through much more places than you could ever imagine."

After a layover in the Netherlands airport for a few hours, my dad and I were in the plane and on our way to Accra, Ghana!

I said good bye to Amsterdam, but I knew that I would be back again...someday! At night in the plane, on our way to Ghana, words could not begin to describe the majestic views that I witnessed in the sky!

In the far distance, you could see massive bolts of lightening coming from the thick clouds. It looked like a light show. The dark, Atlantic waters roared below. I marveled, as I stared outside the window of the plane. What a secret world of nature that Christ had created, hidden from my imagination this entire time.

My eyes had never seen such beauty, such majesty. My heart had never felt so good. I knew that I was truly living in the blessing. I was ready for all the goodness that the Lord had in store for me! Finally, hours later, just around sunset, the plane began its descent into the Ghanaian airport.

Chapter 19

AFRICA: GHANA

Once more, I marveled as I stared out the airplane window. The view was absolutely breathtaking! I felt as if I had traveled to an entirely different planet!

As the plane glided over the Ghanaian terrain, you could see huts in one area and mansions in other areas. You could see seemingly perfect green, manicured landscape, small hills, and valleys. You could see a few vehicles driving below, and livestock grazing through the villages. It looked like a scene that I had watched in an African movie before.

When the plane landed, I looked at my dad with an uncontrollable smile on my face and joy in my heart. After exiting the plane, there it was, that crisp, clean, African air that I had been away from, for two decades! There was nothing like it!

As we walked through the airport, my dad and I were treated like royalty. Security guards ushered us pass the long line. We quickly retrieved our luggage, and headed outside the airport.

Awaiting us smiling, was my mom and my dad's younger brother, my dear Uncle Austin. I smiled. I missed him much! It had been too long since I had seen him as a child in Ghana.

We got in the car and headed directly to my grandfather's home.

"He has been waiting for you, Maubrey. He can't wait to see you!" my mom said to me, still smiling.

The anticipation built. I was the only grandchild left in my huge family, that had not seen my grandfather or grandmother in the twenty years since leaving Africa.

I continued to be amazed as we drove through the bumpy Ghanaian roads. I felt as if I were on a safari ride that night.

Wide-eyed, I marveled at the village people in the streets. I marveled at the homes. I marveled at the music in the air. I was lost in my own little world during that ride.

Finally, we had arrived at my dear grandpa's home! We exited the car, and there he was, slowly approaching us with a cane in his hand and a big smile on his face! It was dark, and his eyes were poor, but he could still see my silhouette.

"Maubrey...! Oh Maubrey!" grandpa exclaimed.

"Grandpa...!" I replied cheerfully, as my parents watched with joy.

The biggest smile shined across my face! I fought hard to hold back tears. I fight even harder to hold back tears now, as I write. This was the man that loved and helped raise me as child, when I barely knew how to tie my shoes, the man that I hid from underneath the table, after my cousins had escaped through the windows of his house. This was the man that every year, for the past 20 years, without fail, had been the first one to send me a birthday card.

An explosion of joy and happiness filled my entire body, as my grandpa and I hugged and embraced one another. I was absolutely amazed, once I got a good look at my grandpa's face. I looked so much like him. And his skin; with the exception of a handful of people, I had never met a person with such radiant, smooth, silky skin. That was my first thought the moment I looked at his face. What a beautiful man!

We went inside his house, took pictures, talked, laughed, prayed, and my grandpa blessed me before leaving that night. It truly was an emotional and glad time for me! We said good bye to my grandpa for the night. We were now on our way to my parents' home. Again, we journeyed through the bumpy roads in town. It was very dark. There were hardly any street signs. I wondered how in the world we were navigating our way to my parents' home.

"We are here." my dad said.

I was in awe! Under the African night skies, we slowly entered a gated community, guarded by security guards with riffles in their hands. I had never seen anything like that in real life!

A guard approached our car to see who we were. Then, they opened the big metal gate to let us into the compound. We drove through the darkness for a few hundred yards into the complex, making some turns, then, finally arrived in the garage of my parents' home.

What a journey I had been on, all the way from Los Angeles, to New Jersey, to Ghana! I had made it! I was finally able to see the home that my parents had been building for the past few years.

I unpacked my bags in my new room, made my bed, and went straight to sleep. I was exhausted, exhausted but in bliss!

Ah… The next morning that I awoke was a morning to remember! Sitting outside on the porch, staring at the African sunrise in the distance was heavenly! That was when it truly hit me where in the world I was! I was in Ghana! I was in Africa! I was home!

But wait…! Now that I have you in Africa with me, hold my hand once again. Open your mind, and time travel with me three years back to the future, to Miami, Florida, where I have been writing the past few chapters to you, tirelessly, for the past two months.

Chapter 20

Christ will not allow me to write another single word in this book of life, without testifying the amazing wonders that occurred just last evening. How I wound up in Miami, from writing to you in a library computer laboratory during the cold, winter days in Belleville, New Jersey will astonish and amaze you in itself. But for now, my testimony leading to last night.

It was one week ago. The scene was South Beach, Miami. I was on the beach, running sprints, training for the 2012 Olympics for the 100 meter and 200 meter, track and field races, believing to break the world record through Christ.

As I kneeled down in starting position and raised my head up to see whether my running lane was clear, I noticed a man who seemed to be in his late twenties to early thirties. He paused to give me room to sprint on the sand, before crossing my path to go into the warm beach waters.

As I walked back to my starting position after sprinting past him, he greeted me and asked me, as many by passers had, during the past two months of training on the beach, whether I was training for something.

"Yeah," I responded, "I'm training for the Olympics."

"That's great! Many blessings!" he said.

I noticed that instead of going into the ocean, he decided to sit on the beach and watch, as I ran. I walked back to my starting position and sprinted past him once again. As I walked back, he started a brief conversation with me.

During our conversation, he spoke of how the Lord Jesus had saved his life. Afterwards, he invited me to his church. He also spoke of how amazing the church he attended was, and how they performed spiritual healings on a regular basis, and how they believed in the unexplainable, supernatural power of Christ. He also said that it was a mega church with over 6,000 congregation members.

I was more than happy to accept his invitation, since I hadn't been to a church in the two months that I had been in Miami. We exchanged contact information, then, I finally went back to my training, and he finally went to swim in the ocean. About an hour later, we shook hands before he left, and agreed to meet for church on the weekend.

Last evening, at around 6:00 P.M., Sunday, he and two other new friends of his, a mid twenties, Dominican Republic fellow countryman of his, and an older, but youthful looking Peruvian woman in her late sixties, arrived to pick me up to church services. I could feel a positive energy from the moment that I entered the car.

During the half an hour ride to the church, I testified of how reading Deuteronomy 28: 1-13, just minutes before they picked me up, had inspired me to write my first song since arriving in Miami. I knew in my heart, that it would be a hit song, thus we rejoiced and praised the Lord.

He later spoke of how this church would forever change my life. I was intrigued and open. We finally arrived in front of the mega church and parked the car.

One thing that I cannot leave out is that, it had been pouring, raining all day and even during the drive to the church, however I seem to have been the only one that noticed that the moment we came within a few minutes away from the church, traffic had cleared.

The rain had suddenly ceased. The dark, grey clouds parted, as Moses had parted the Red Sea. Blue skies appeared. The Lord shined the sun's warm rays brightly upon our faces! We parked and entered the mega church.

You could feel an electric energy from the moment that you walked into the worship auditorium! There was music! There were cameras! There were beautiful, lavender and light blue lighting on the stage! The church ceiling was many stories high! The seats were filled to capacity!

For the next few hours, we worshiped, prayed, sang songs, and listened to the pastor preach. The night was remarkable! In the middle of the sermon, the pastor asked all the married couples who were willing, to come up on the stage.

He said a prayer for them. Then, as the married couples held hands on the stage, he asked all the single people in the church who were willing, to approach the front of the church.

My new friends, Henry, Cooper, and I went forth. When all were in front of the church, we were asked to raise our hands up high in the air and to pray to the Lord, Jesus, for our needs and tribulations that we were facing in life.

I witnessed people praying on their knees. I witnessed men and women crying. I witnessed pure faith! Christ was certainly in our presence!

A younger man in front of me was weeping heavily. I put my hand on his shoulder. I could feel his pain. When we finished praying, he turned around, and I gave him a hug.

"It's OK…" I said to him, "It's OK…"

We then returned to our seats. The pastor preached for some time more. At the end of the sermon, the pastor said that all new members of the church of the over 6,000 in attendance should come forward to the stage.

The Journey to The Kingdom of Heaven

At first, I watched as dozens of people walked forward from their seats. I had no intention of going forward to the front of the church, in front of thousands of people.

But then, Henry said to me, "You should go, brother. It's very important."

"OK. Sure." I said without hesitation.

"Why not?" I thought to myself.

So, from the rear of the massive church, I began my stride, walking over 100 feet, all the way to the front of the church.

When I got to the front of the church, there was a straight line of all the first time members facing the pastor, who was on the stage. I was ushered to join the line. Our backs were turned to the sea of congregation members, as they listened to the pastor warmly welcome and congratulate us for coming forward.

Suddenly, I noticed to my left, that dozens of church volunteers, all wearing matching red t-shirts with the churches logo on them, began to run behind us from the left to the right end of the line that we had formed. I smiled. I wondered what they would be doing behind us. I imagined that they would be instructed by the pastor to bless us through their touch.

From the stage, the pastor said a brief prayer for us, and then instructed us to turn around and greet the volunteer members behind us.

Suddenly, we were instructed by the pastor to be led into another room of the massive church. Suddenly, I heard the congregation erupt in cheer and applaud! I faced my left to go, and then suddenly again, I found myself in the front of the line.

I knew that just seconds ago, there were a handful of new members to my left. I immediately wondered where they had vanished to. Then, the thought left my mind. As we made our way outside of the church auditorium and into the hallway, the congregation erupted once more with claps and cheers.

As one church volunteer and I led the other new members into the hallway, we were greeted by dozens of members with more clapping, applauding, and jubilation, as angels and ancestors would do at your entrance into the Kingdom of Heaven – as if I had just won the lottery – as if I had just won a championship – as if I were in an extravagant parade!

I had never felt that feeling in my life before! The excitement on their faces – the joy in their big, bright smiles! There was a man with a video camera in front of me. Another man waved a big, solid purple flag, the exact same color of the fitted v-neck shirt that I was wearing.

We were lead in a hurry through the hallways, as the cheers continued. It was remarkable! I smiled and clapped as well.

Finally, we entered a classroom sized room. When everyone entered the room, the lights were shut off, and a projection screen appeared in front of the room. It was a prerecorded video of the head minister speaking in Spanish.

I could not understand the language, however, I could tell that he was congratulating us on taking the step towards Jesus, and welcoming us to the church.

When the video ended, the lights were turned on and then all in the room clapped their hands. A junior minister, who must have been in his early thirties, then walked onto the one foot high podium in front of the room to speak to us.

He began to speak in Spanish. I felt a bit left out, since I did not understand Spanish. But I worried not.

"First of all, who in here," he interrupted, "Does not understand Spanish?"

In the room of over 50 people, I and one other person were the only ones who raised our hands. The minister looked into my direction.

"Ok." he said with a smile, "I'll try and speak Spanglish."

He also instructed another church member to come by my side to translate what was going to be said in the room to me.

The minister welcomed us and began to speak. He told us that for us to see firsthand, the glory of Jesus, he would let the three people behind him, step up to the podium and testify about the recent miracles in their lives.

The first man stepped up to the podium. He began to testify in Spanish. My translator translated as the man spoke. The man testified that not long ago, he was driving his vehicle when he accidentally hit a school bus full of students. He continued to drive, thinking that there was no damage and that only his side view mirror had grazed the bus. He said that he had later been arrested for hit-and-run, and that the charges were much more severe, since it involved a school bus full of children.

He said that when he went to the court, that there were dozens of witnesses there to testify against him. He spoke of how he prayed tirelessly to the Lord Jesus and asked the elders of the church to pray for him as well.

Lo and behold, when he returned to court one day, the judge told him to go home! The charges had been completely dropped! He praised the Lord.

That testimony sounded incredibly familiar to me!

Another woman stepped up to the podium with her son. She spoke of how her son's eyes had been filled with puss and was severely infected to the point that he could not see out of both eyes anymore. She took her son to see many doctors. All the doctors said that they could not treat him. She testified that within three days of speaking with the ministers of the church and praying to Jesus, her son was miraculously cured!

That sounded incredibly familiar to me!

The last testimony came from an older gentleman who said that his brother in California had had two heart attacks in a short amount of time. He had to fly from Miami to California to visit his brother. He testified that upon returning to Miami and receiving the prayers and support from the congregation, his brother had recovered and had been doing well ever since! He praised the Lord!

That sounded incredibly familiar to me!

The old gentleman stepped down from the podium. Then the minister stepped back up to the podium. The minister began to speak. He told us that at this time, if any of us had any muscular or bodily pains, ministers would come to each of us and pray for healing.

For about a minute, the minister who was assigned to me prayed for healing of my neck and trapezoid muscle that had been aching me since my days of wrestling in high school. I thanked and hugged him for the prayer of healing.

Afterwards, the main minister who had been speaking on the podium began to speak again. He congratulated us once again for making a covenant with Christ. He told us that he was going to perform a final prayer before we left.

Just as we began to bow our heads in prayer, the miraculous happened! My destiny began to unfold!

The minister on the podium, out of the entire packed room, looked at me and pointed to me.

"You, come up brother. I'm going to pray for you!"

I looked around briefly to make sure he was pointing at me. He was. I smiled and laughed in my head for a moment.

"Why am I not surprised?" I thought.

I gracefully walked up to the podium.

"Please bow your heads." the minister instructed the room.

He placed his palm on the crown of my head and began to pray for me in front of the entire room. I recall him thanking the Lord for bringing me into their presence, from a faraway place. He had no idea that I had journeyed to Miami, all the way from New Jersey. He prayed that I will touch and heal the world! He prayed that I would prophesy to the nations. He prayed that I would be a true inspiration to all that know me.

My hands suddenly lifted to the sky! The minister prayed that I would cast out demons and bring glory to the Kingdom of Christ! He asked Jesus to use me, His child, for good in the world!

"How does the minister know what is in my heart?" I thought to myself.

My spirit was ignited! I almost began to weep as I stretched my hands higher to the heavens. Unaware, my state of mind had changed.

"...In the name of Jesus!" the minister exclaimed, as he removed his hands from my head.

What happened immediately after, was a miracle indeed! The moment the minister exclaimed, "In the name of Jesus!" and removed his palm from my head, I became semiconscious, and the Holy Spirit flashed from the heavens and entered into my mind, body and heart!

It was nothing like I had ever felt before, in my entire existence! With my hands still in the sky, and my eyes shut closed, almost in slow motion, I began to faint backwards, as if it were a dream.

The surreal thing was that, I had lost consciousness to the outside world, however, in my head, I was completely conscious. I could still hear, feel, and smell everything in the room.

The first thing that came to mind, as I slowly began to fall backwards, was, "Is this really happening to me? Am I really fainting in front of all these complete strangers?"

In the past, I had seen on television and a few times in church, many men and women fainting after the touch and prayer of the Lord. I always thought that they either were told to faint after the prayer, that they were pretending to faint, or that they were simply over dramatic. I never imagined that the Holy Spirit of Christ had actually entered their bodies.

My friend, I can testify that He is as real as the air you breathe! Christ will come, if your gates of faith are wide open and you let Him in!

Just before I hit the ground, I felt the gentle arms of two or three people behind me, catching me to break my fall. I could feel them laying me gently, flat on my back on the floor.

My arms still, were stretched out on the floor, over my head. Immediately, I felt someone place two warm blankets over my body, from my chest down. My eyes began to twitch, letting in quick flashes of light and images in the room. The entire room surrounded my motionless body.

The minister stepped down from the podium. He continued to bless and anoint me as I laid semiconscious on my back.

I heard people gasp! I heard people cry! As the minister prayed, that is when I saw the Divine Light! I was transported to a euphoric state of being! My eyes continued to twitch. My jaws were relaxed. And my lips were closed.

I decided to let go, and allow Jesus Christ to take control of my mind, body and spirit! I felt a tranquil sense of peace. Then, the Lord began to speak to me! My heart raced. My chest began to shake lightly! His words were as clear as day.

My heavenly Father said to me: "My son, this is it! I am real! Hear My voice! You are chosen! Every dream that I had ever given you, from the time you were a child will come to fruition! I will hold nothing back from you! You will change the world! You will inspire the world! You will bring comfort and hope to those in greatest need! I will use you, My son, to give to the world! I will use you, My son, to change the world and bring all to the Kingdom of Heaven! Maubrey, every moment of your life, all that you have been through, was masterfully designed by Me, to bring you out of New Jersey to Miami, for you to be training on the beach on that fateful day. I brought Henry across your path so that he may bring you here, so that you may arrive at this very moment to meet Me! This entire night, these thousands of people in My house of worship, was perfectly architected for you, Maubrey! I brought you here, that I may show Myself to you for the first time! I did not want to show Myself while you were conscious. I did not want to show Myself in your dreams. I wanted to enter your mind and conscience at this very moment in time, so that there be no doubt as to what you are now seeing and experiencing! Go forth Maubrey, and let My will be done on Earth!"

For the following moments, I could hear the minister continue to passionately bless me as I laid on my back.

Wonders continued! He had been preaching in Spanish the majority of the time. I do not understand Spanish. But suddenly, I was beginning to understand some of the words that he was speaking!

I heard him say something about Los Angeles. I believe I heard him saying something about my life as a former drug lord, years ago. I believe I heard him say something about my business. I believe I heard him say something about my childhood.

My eyes continued to twitch, and my chest began to shake more. How was it that the minister was preaching about my past? I knew that the Lord Jesus was speaking through him!

Finally, the minister finished blessing me. I thought I would automatically regain consciousness and mobility in my body. I was wrong.

Jesus said to me: "I'm not going to wake you up, Maubrey. You must wake yourself up."

Finally, I heard and felt members of the group calling me and holding my hand to lift me up, and with a turn of time, I awoke!

Yes...! I awoke!

I sat up, and then was helped up to my feet. I was still slightly dazed, and amazed by the miracle that had just happened. What had just happened to me was better than any drug in the world! It was better than the feeling of sex! It was better than falling in love with a beautiful woman!

I had fallen in love with Jesus all over again! After helping me to my feet, the minister gave me a big, warm hug.

He looked me directly in the eyes and said, "You will do all the things that are in your heart, but you can't do it without Christ."

"I believe!" I humbly replied.

"You see," the minister said, "I did not know anything about you, except that they told me your name."

"Destined!" he exclaimed.

"Wow, what a name...! Destined for greatness...!"

He told me that he was Minister Alex. I humbly thanked him for the blessing. A few other church members hugged me.

"Welcome home!" one of them said.

I was home indeed...! I was home indeed...!

Chapter 21

Travel now, back with me through the vortex of time. The year is 2007. The scene is Ghana.

I recall sitting on the porch that first morning, smelling that fresh African air, viewing that magnificent African sunrise.

Breakfast was extraordinary! The food in Ghana was so fresh. Even the eggs tasted completely different than the eggs I had been eating for the majority of my life in America.

I also can't forget the taste of the freshly baked butter bread that the Ghanaian women would sell door to door from a flat board resting on the top of their heads. It was just like I had seen on television all my life.

Just a few steps across, was my aunt's home that was under development. Another few steps to the right, was my two cousins' that we had grown up with, while living in Ghana, beautiful, luxurious home.

My parents took me sightseeing all around town that first morning. I was amazed at all that I saw! The smiles and happiness of my country people were inspiring. Many of them lived far below standards, however, they still had great joy in their faces.

I can't forget how bumpy most of the roads were. I always used to joke that it felt like we were on a safari during the drives. There were not typical road signs. I remember being so confused whenever we would go somewhere. I wondered how people were able to navigate, especially at night.

Also, the neighborhoods were in such contrast. On one plot of land, I would see a luxurious mansion, and then just a few feet away, I would see rundown huts. I immediately realized the development and transformation for the better, that was taking place.

It seemed that there were Christian symbols, Bible verses, and paintings of Christ on nearly every building and home that I saw. There was no doubt that my homeland was blessed!

On the radio and television, I joked that it seemed like all they spoke about was armed robbers breaking into people's homes, or about something related to the president of the country. I loved the music that surrounded me!

"Burger Fresh!" some local teenager relaxing on the side of the road shouted at me with a smile on his face, as I stared wide-eyed, out of the car window.

I asked my parents what that meant.

"Oh, that means that they can tell that you are a foreigner that is new in town."

My nickname became "Burger Fresh" for the remainder of my vacation. I laughed each time a family member would call me that.

The adorable Ghanaian children inspired me the most. I remember stopping at the side of the road to give them some change in my pocket. They dashed to the car. They were so excited! They were so innocent! They were such pure believers! I miss them dearly for the way they touched my heart.

A few nights after I had arrived, finally, it was time to go to my eldest aunt's 60th birthday celebration, where the entire family, most of which I had not seen in years, including my grandma, who I had not seen in 20 years, were going to be!

We arrived at the celebration later than the rest of the family. Oh, how my heart was filled with great joy the moment I saw my wonderful and vibrant grandmother! We kissed and hugged for so long! We couldn't help looking at each other in the eyes and smiling, like we had a special bond when I was a child. I missed her dearly! What a wonderful night to remember!

I also got to see my cousins and aunts that I hadn't seen for so long. I got to see other cousins, uncles and aunts that I had never met before.

We danced, we ate, we drank, and we celebrated all night long! I especially loved how energetic and lively I discovered my grandma was. There was no doubt as to where my happiness originated from!

And then, another priceless highlight of my night certainly was being able to see my "baby", my cousin Lily's daughter, my niece that I loved more than the world itself, when they came from London to visit my other cousin Hannah in Tallahassee, Florida, during that one summer in high school.

The last time I saw her, my darling niece, Zoe was but a toddler. And now, she was all grown up! It made my day, by the sparkle in her eyes when she looked at me, and the fact that she followed me wherever I went, never leaving my side after reuniting, to know that she loved me so much. I loved her even more!

The family reunion continued during my stay in Ghana. Another day, I was reunited with my older, half brother from my father's side.

Days later, I was reunited with my half sister, and her children, also from my father's side.

The Lord had reunited me with nearly all my entire family. I was truly blessed indeed! I recall a somber time of my visit, when we were driving in a rural village area. My dad was told that his brother, my uncle, was not well. I assumed that he was slightly ill.

However, when we arrived at his home, my first time meeting him since arriving in Ghana, I witnessed my father break down into tears after a few moments of attempting to communicate with his older brother. I comforted my uncle and my dad as he wept.

The villagers could not figure out what was wrong with my uncle. It seemed to me that he had symptoms of dementia. A short while later, some other family members and the village king, who I later was told was in the process of being dethroned, gathered together to discuss other problems and concerns in the village, and to offer advice and give suggestions on the best way to help my uncle.

As we sat in a circle, I suggested that they continually play good, nostalgic music, to keep my uncle in good spirits, allowing him to gradually come back to normal.

Afterwards, the elders decided that we should all hold hands and pray for my uncle. I followed about a dozen of them, including my parents, a few yards from where we were sitting, to a small shack. Inside the dark shack was a wooden idol!

We held hands, bowed our heads, and listened as an elder began to pray in our native tongue.

At that time, just beginning to read the Bible weeks before, I was virtually clueless, as to the terrible sin of praying to, and worshiping a wooden image, but something deep down inside me, made me incredibly uneasy!

My heart began to beat rapidly! I did not know what it was at the time, but I knew that something was just not right! I closed my eyes, tuned out the elder who was praying, and then asked Jesus to heal my uncle.

Soon after talking to Jesus and returning to our seats, it hit me what had just happened! I sat there quietly, realizing that the members of the village were not of Christ, but were idol worshipers!

For the first time in my life, I realized that my father was not a Christian, and that my mom was not fully converted. It was an astonishing revelation that the Lord had waited over two decades to reveal to me! I love and honor both of my earthly parents, unconditionally and regardless.

I pray confidently, that one day, they will never again worship or pray to an idol or false god again. I can see my dad, my mom, and the rest of my family standing on a stage in front of an ocean of people, testifying about the powerful day that they became fully saved by Jesus Christ, the Son of God! I can see it happening clearly in my vision of faith!

I immediately realized the source of all the problems in that village. They were worshiping other gods! They were worshiping idols!

I recall later, being asked by someone, as we sat and spoke, if I would like to be made king of their tribe. I told them that I would have to carefully consider it and let them know in the future. But in my mind, I was thinking that the only way that I would ever be king over the people, was if all the idols were destroyed and if they were willing and open to fully convert to the Son of God, Jesus Christ!

Another day, my parents took me to finally visit my grandmother's house that I grew up in. How wonderful it was! It brought back so many fond memories. It looked so different from what I remembered two decades ago though. The house seemed a lot smaller than I remembered. A lot had changed in 20 years. My parents and I took photographs, and met some neighbors and family that I had grown up with, who I did not remember. They however, seemed to remember me quite well.

It was a very humbling experience! It made me realize how much my parents had done for me all my life and how far I had come!

Another day, my parents woke me up very early in the morning to see my father's home that he had been building for years. After driving deep into the rural area for what seemed to be ages, we arrived at the compound.

The estate was massive! I was amazed! I began to realize why my parents had been frugal and humble with their money for all those years growing up. They had been planning for their future. They had been planning for my siblings and my future.

Things were beginning to become clearer and clearer as my days in Ghana passed by. I was learning so much.

The remainder of my two week visit to Ghana was full of excitement! One of my older cousins, who I grew up with in Ghana, flew in from London a few days after I had arrived. It was great to see him after so many years. I remembered the times when I was only 4 years old, living in Ghana. My cousin and his brother were almost teenagers. We used to play pillow fight on the bed. We had so much fun growing up together for those short years.

Now, we were all grown up. We had seen the world. We had been through so much. My cousin had been flying back and forth from London to Ghana over the years, so he was familiar with all the areas in town. He took me to almost every exciting nightclub and restaurants in town every night. He treated me amazingly! It was good to be together again.

I can't forget how many countless times we would get home after 5 A.M. in the morning, intoxicated with wine. I always insisted on drinking wine only, whenever I would drink.

Upon returning from a night out, my cousin would go into his house, directly across from my parents' house. I would knock on the side windows of my parents' house, smiling from ear to ear, and wake them, or our housekeeper up to let me in.

Half asleep, they would always laugh and shake their heads. They knew that I was having the time of my life, enjoying the blessing of being back in my homeland.

And then, at 23 years of age, after having sex with dozens of women in college, there was the first time that I had had sex with a black woman! I recall my cousin and his friend taking me out one night to a nightclub. I must have had about four or five glasses of red wine with them.

Then, they decided to take me to another side of town that evening, to go to a different bar. 'Jokers' was the name of the bar. I can't forget. We pulled up and parked directly in front of the bar. I was extremely intoxicated. I remember following my cousin and his friends into the bar with a euphoric feeling inside my body, and a cheerful look on my face.

As I followed my party in from behind, less than 10 seconds after entering the bar, I noticed a woman giving me a very seductive look into my eyes. I had definitely seen that look many times before.

Before my cousins and his friends even realized, the woman came straight to me, pinned me against the wall, and began speaking extremely sexually to me. I could not resist that Ghanaian accent!

Seconds later, we were caressing one another's bodies and locking lips. My cousin and his friends had absolutely no idea that I was no longer following behind them. I grabbed her hand and led her right back out to the car that we had just parked a few feet from the front of the bar. I smiled and winked at the doorman as we exited the bar.

He smiled back and shook his head as if he was thinking, "Didn't he just come inside the bar just seconds ago?"

We went straight to the back seat of the car and ripped off one another's clothes. I quickly put on a condom and began to have sex with the voluptuous woman from Nigeria. I smiled inside.

I thought to myself as I went into her, "This must be a record for me!"

With all my wild and crazy nights in Indiana University and Los Angeles, I've never had sex with a woman within minutes of meeting her in a bar or nightclub!

After a few minutes of having sex with the woman in the backseat of the car, we heard knocking on the car door, laughter outside, and felt the car shaking and rocking. By then, the car windows were completely steamed and fogged.

It was my cousin, his friends and security guards that had surrounded the car in laughter, and were rocking it from side to side. The security guards must have told them that I was in the car having sex with the Nigerian woman. I smile and shake my head, as I think of the night.

I still remember her sweet African accent. We tried our best to continue having sex, as the car rocked from side to side. The scene was quite comical.

Finally, we finished having sex. I unlocked the car doors and stepped outside with a huge smile on my face. I saw my cousin, friends, and security guards dying of laughter.

They probably had never seen something like that before. I remember reentering the car as the woman dressed. She asked me for money to pay for minutes for her cell phone. I learned that that was Ghanaians' form of prostitution. Instead of asking for money, they asked for help to pay for cell phone minutes.

"Don't give her any money!" my cousin said to me.

I felt bad and was unsure of what to do. I wasn't sure if she genuinely needed the money, or if she used that tactic every time she had sex with a man.

I remember my cousin's friend soon distracting her by cleverly leading her away from the car that I had arrived in. Seconds later, my cousin and I were dashing to the car and speeding off into the night. What a night in Africa! Alcohol, women, sex, and adventure!

My cousin and his friends had been trying all along to set me up with my first African woman, and it finally happened when they least expected it. They laughed and retold that story for the remainder of my vacation.

Then, there was the second time I had sex with an African woman. A friend of my cousin had taken me to a nightclub late one evening. After a long fun night, and a few glasses of wine, we exited the nightclub.

Across the street was a group of women. A tall, slender woman with a sexy, bright red dress immediately caught my eye. We made eye contact. She must have been about 19 or 20 years old. I knew that I had to approach her and talk with her. My hormones were raging! She was one of the most beautiful women that I had ever seen in my life!

After I approached her, we began to flirt, talking sexually to one another. I can't forget her enchanting, almond shaped eyes! Within seconds, I was leading her to my friend's car that we had come in.

"This is too easy." I thought to myself with a smile.

However, I still had the memory of the Nigerian woman that I had had sex with about a week before, so I wasn't too surprised. We got into the car, and just as I did with the Nigerian woman, we started aggressively undressing one another. I can still remember her sweet Ghanaian accent. It was like listening to an angel speak!

Just after she completely undressed me, and she was in nothing but her underwear, she put a halt to the flow.

"I'm going to need money." she said.

I was absolutely dumbfounded! This beautiful woman had caught me completely off guard!

"Don't worry about money..." I said, in attempt to persuade her.

But she held her ground. My cousins had warned me earlier, that a lot of beautiful women at nightclubs would ask for money for sex.

All my life, I swore to myself that I would never pay a woman to have sex with her. Now, here I was, on top of one of the most beautiful African woman that I had ever seen, almost completely nude, her enchanting dove eyes peering deep into mine, her long, black flowing, silky hair resting on the back seat, and her sweet accent melting my heart. I was trapped in lust!

For the next 20 minutes or so, I tried all the tricks that I had been using to seduce women into having sex, ever since I was 18 years old. I talked and talked and talked. I offered her the world. I painted a fantasy future. I told her that I loved her. I rubbed my hard abs and chest against her skin.

Nothing...! This woman did not budge!

"I need money to pay for a taxi and for minutes for my phone." she said, once again with that honey sweet accent.

I could not resist. She had enchanted me! Finally, I reached into my wallet. I pulled out $5 dollars and told her that that was all that I had.

She said it wasn't enough. My heart burned with sexual frustration. I pulled out about $20 dollars more. Still, she said it was not enough.

"I've never done this before," she said, again in that angelic voice. "The only reason I'm doing this is because I just broke up with my boyfriend, and now, I need money for transportation and mobile phone minutes."

I practically begged and pleaded, giving her my most innocent face that I had. I had met my match! This Ghanaian girl was good! Her strength actually turned me on the more! No woman in my 23 short years of being on this earth, had ever been able to convince me to give her a single penny for sex.

Finally, I surrendered to her. I reached into my wallet and handed her all the $70 dollars in cash that I had.

"Are we going to your house?" she asked.

Only now, as I write, do I realize that she may have been telling the truth that she's never done such things. Perhaps, she thought that I was going to drive her to my house and just wanted money beforehand to be sure that she could get back home, or at least call someone for a ride.

Or, perhaps, I'm just being naive. After all, taxi rides are so inexpensive in Ghana. It only costs about $5 dollars to travel about 40 miles in a taxi.

"We can have sex here." I replied, referring to the ever familiar back seat.

I watched as she slowly rolled the condom on my penis. Then, I went inside of her and had passionate sex for some time, before the condom suddenly broke!

To be honest, I thought that the condom might have broken much earlier. I think she felt the same. But we kept going. Something in my mind was telling me that if she had my child, I would not mind. I had fallen in love with this tall, dark, beautiful, exotic, Ghanaian girl so easily – so fast.

By the time we had finished having sex, my cousin's friend was there smiling outside the car. We got dressed, exchanged numbers, and took her to her friends just a few blocks away.

My friend and I drove away. I never heard from, or saw that beautiful, tall, Ghanaian woman again.

Sometimes, I wonder...

It was also in Ghana, where I saw one of the most beautiful, tall women that I had ever seen in my 23 years of living.

I can't forget this other woman. She stood at about 6 feet tall, about 6'3" inches with high heel shoes. Her face was absolutely flawless. Her hair was long, black and silky. She had rich, dark chocolate, creamy skin. Her body was divine!

The first time I laid eyes on this woman, I looked at my cousin, who, as I had mentioned earlier, had been unsuccessfully trying to set me up with Ghanaian women since he arrived. I was just too selective. I was willing to be patient.

"That's the one!" I said to my cousin with a smile.

The woman and I made eye contact a few times, so I decided to join her at her table as she waited on a date. I tried to engage in a conversation with her, however I was shut down. I swallowed my pride and walked back to my cousin's table after a while.

I remember seeing the same woman, nights later, after leaving a nightclub. I approached her again. The only thing I could think of asking this exotic beauty was whether she was interested in modeling in the U.S.

"I'm not interested." she quickly replied.

I was completely turned down again! It was then, that I realized that she must be approached by so many men daily, wanting only one thing from her. Sex. I realized that I should have just been myself as usual, and started a decent conversation with the angel. I never saw her again, after that night. I surely learned a lesson that evening.

I definitely enjoyed the nightlife and entertainment in Ghana. From the hotel parties, to the fine restaurants, to the nightclubs, I take with me some amazing fond memories!

I remember there being black outs in Ghana, almost every day, even at some nightclubs, but the party still kept going until an electrical generator was activated. It was surreal to see that they played hit music by American musicians like Lil' Wayne and 50 Cent.

I was dazzled by the views of horseback riders from the beachside nightclubs, as the waves from the Atlantic Ocean pounded in the picturesque background.

On my last full day in Ghana, under beautiful, picture perfect, sunny skies, I took a long, peaceful walk alone. I went into my own world. I marveled at the beauty and majesty of the land and people. I toured local shops and art galleries. I became lost in the atmosphere. I soaked in all that my country had to offer; all the culture, all the heritage, all the history, all the sounds.

In the background, I could hear the sound of Michael Jackson's music playing smoothly and clearly in the air. I truly felt at home! I truly felt happy! However, I was sad to have to leave my homeland. What a wonderful land! I had been through so much in the short two weeks that I was in Ghana. I had been on quite an adventure. I learned so much about the world. I learned so much about myself.

I would dearly miss Ghana; the food, the weather, the women, the people, the dancing, the music, the celebration, the love!

Once again, my journey to the Kingdom of Heaven continued! Good bye Ghana! Good Bye Africa! Until we meet again…!

Chapter 22

THE GARDEN STATE

I arrived back in New Jersey with a new vision, a new perspective of life. The trip to Africa had opened my eyes. It made me realize that there was so much to do. It made me understand that I could not fail. People were in great need. I had to do my part to give more and help more!

Once again in my life, the Lord had put things into clear perspective. I had a new fire burning inside my heart!

The irony is that I had absolutely no money or savings going to Ghana, and upon returning from Ghana, however I knew in my heart that I had to move forward. Returning to live in Los Angeles became less likely.

Upon my return from Africa, I learned that all of my life's possessions that I had stored in the storage unit had been auctioned off for a total of $25 dollars! Thousands and thousands of dollars of clothes, electronics, furniture, jewelry, priceless photographs, and the cherished art piece that I had bought from the 16 year old Moroccan boy, all gone to the highest bidder for $25 dollars.

My heart dropped as the woman on the other end of the phone broke the news to me. But I could not get upset. I knew that it was my fault for not paying the monthly fees. I had given the storage company $1 dollar for the first month, and now, all of my possessions were gone within a blink of an eye.

I wanted to return to Los Angeles, however, this proved that the Lord Jesus had much different plans for my life.

Looking back, I realize that the Lord's plans are always much more magnificent and greater than anything I could ever even imagine! The Lord had literally given me a fresh start. He had supernaturally rid me of all the possessions that I had acquired through sin. It was a new day! It was a brand new beginning! The Lord had begun a new work inside of me! My true, divine powers would have to come out, should I not only survive, but prosper abundantly!

I had to take a step back from the world once again to analyze my life. I had to tune my mind with the frequency of Jesus.

I knew that I did not want to work a 9-5 job. I had been selling drugs for so long, that, that was all I knew. But those days were long and gone!

I remember going to New York's, Union Square the week after returning to the U.S. to sell Ghanaian masks that my parents had given me money to invest in, while I was in Ghana.

I bought them for about $3 dollars each, and figured that I could sell them for about $100 dollars each. If I sold all 20 or so masks for $100 dollars each, then I would make $2000 dollars from expenses of only about $60 dollars. Those were the kind of profits that I was used to.

So every day, for about a week, I would wake up very early in the morning and take a carry-on luggage full of masks from my parents' home in Belleville, New Jersey to Union Square in New York City.

I took my Bible with me and began reading from the very beginning again. I met a lot of good people that week, but I don't recall selling any masks.

Then one day, during the week, a merchant who was selling African cloths and masks approached me, offering to sell all my masks on consignment. I would give him all my masks, he would give me a small deposit for good faith, and then, he would pay me daily as he sold the masks.

I saw this as a miracle! No longer would I have to wake up early in the morning, travel all the way from New Jersey to New York, and spend all day trying to make sales.

I agreed. Within a few weeks, all the masks were sold, and I was given about $20 dollars for each mask. It wasn't quite as much as I expected, but still, it was almost a 1000% profit on my initial investment.

My mind began to do calculations. I contemplated being an importer of African art. But it just was not for me. Christ had bigger plans for my life – much bigger plans!

After spending a few weeks living at my parents' home in New Jersey, upon returning from Africa, I moved in with my brother, first, to where he was living in Gramercy Park, New York City, and then to Soho, New York City.

My brother, who had been making a living as a personal trainer at the time, was training a fairly wealthy client who owned properties throughout Manhattan. I was a bit lost and undecided as to what I was going to do to survive in New York City.

The little money that I had made from selling the masks was gone. I had to depend on my brother for food and transportation.

In Soho, we lived in the basement of a vacant, high-end retail store on Green Street. I remember there being no shower, so we had to shower after working out at a local gym.

Those first few weeks were a constant struggle. How ironic my situation was. I was living in a $10,000,000 dollar plus building, in one of the most affluent neighborhoods in the country, Soho, in one of the greatest cities in the world, New York, yet I had barley any money in my bank account to eat.

I decided to follow my brother's footsteps, and went to all the high end gyms to apply to become a personal trainer.

However, despite my peak physical form and knowledge about health and wellness, I was turned down by the handful of gyms that I interviewed with. What was the reason? The Lord had other plans for me.

Weeks later, I went to open calls for all the top 10 modeling agencies in New York City. Again, I was rejected, one by one.

They all told me the same thing – that my look was beautiful, strong, and unique, but that I was just not what they were looking for at the time.

I could not understand at the time. I asked God what he wanted out of me. The answer was patience.

In the mean time, I continued to go out to the top New York City, celebrity nightclubs, networking with as many people as possible, searching for that one opportunity and celebrating at the same time.

It was only by the grace and favor of Jesus, that I was able to survive for about a month in New York City with hardly any finances.

Then there was the time I slept on the streets of the Financial District in Manhattan.

It was the first week of October. My 24th birthday had arrived. My brother and I had gone out with a woman that he was dating at the time, and a visiting girlfriend of hers from Brazil.

Judging by the sexual looks that the Brazilian woman was giving me, I imagined it was going to be another wild birthday.

People bought me drink after drink. Before long, I found myself and the Brazilian woman, passionately kissing in the nightclub, while dancing sexually and close. The night went on.

Later, I wandered away (as I usually do), celebrating and dancing with other women. Then, I received a text message from my brother who was in another area of the nightclub, telling me that he and the women were leaving the nightclub. He wanted me to meet him and the two women outside.

Still celebrating inside for a bit longer, by the time I got outside, I realized that they had already taken a taxi to the apartment of the woman my brother was dating, in the exclusive Financial District of Manhattan.

Very intoxicated, the first thing that came to my mind was that I had to rush there to have sex with the sexual Brazilian woman. I hailed the first taxi cab that I could find and was on my way! My hormones climbed by the second, thinking of having sex with this woman.

Minutes later, I had arrived in the area where the woman lived. However, my brother had not given me a clear address and apartment number. He too, probably as much as me, was extremely intoxicated as well.

I called his cell phone once. There was no answer. I called again. Still, no answer. I began to get frustrated, sexually frustrated.

All I could think in my intoxicated state of mind, was my brother having sex with both his lady friend and the Brazilian woman at the same time – without me. I would not put that past him.

My heart burned with lust. I was so close, yet I had no clear address. I recognized the location, as my brother and I had visited her home days before.

Finally, after unsuccessfully attempting to reach my brother an endless amount of times, I decided to go into the lobby of the luxurious, high-rise building. I described my party to the doorman.

He seemed to have remembered a group fitting the description coming in earlier, but also did not have an exact apartment number. He told me to feel free to check the floor that I thought they were in.

Into the elevator I went. In my drunken state, I believe I got out on one of the higher floors. With the anticipation of sex on my birthday in my lustful heart, I wondered through the hallways of this high end, ultra-luxury, Manhattan building.

Late that evening, now around 3 A.M., I must have knocked on door after door. No one answered. I am surprised that the police weren't called.

Finally, sexually frustrated, and in more heat than ever before, I found an apartment with the door opened.

"This is her apartment!" I foolishly thought to myself.

I entered what turned out to be a massive, multiple bedroom, multiple story loft. In my intoxicated state of mind, with my vision slightly impaired, the place seemed like a maze to me. I stumbled from room to room, and remember climbing staircases inside of the apartment, calling out the girls' and my older brother's name aloud, and stumbling into the kitchen, living room, and bathrooms!

Just thinking back now, I shake my head, thinking of how daring and foolish I was. I was determined for sex!

Finally, a guy around the same age as me, in his mid twenties appeared in his boxers, half asleep.

"Dude, what are you doing here?" he asked with great confusion.

Slurring most of my words, I explained my entire dilemma to him. He must have figured that I was harmless and that I was telling the truth.

Looking back again, I thank the Lord for His divine protection over His foolish child! Had it not been for His protection, I could have easily been killed for being in complete strangers' home, late that evening.

I could have been stabbed with a knife, clubbed with a bat, or shot with a gun.

The things that sex and alcohol will do to man...

"Wrong apartment, bro..." he said, half asleep.

He led me out of the apartment, down the elevator, and into the lobby. He must have told the doorman that I was in his apartment.

Just minutes after attempting to contact my brother on his cell phone again, the doorman informed me that I could not stay inside the lobby. I politely obliged.

It's sad to say, but for the next hour, I sat right in front of the building, calling and calling my brother. It's amazing how much sex was in the forefront of my mind. I had never seen myself like that before.

Perhaps, it was a combination of it being my 24th birthday, the fact that I was extremely intoxicated, and the frustration of feeling as if my brother had deserted me for women. My heart burned and burned as that night went by!

Finally, after about an hour of repeated calls and tears of frustration and hurt, I cried myself to sleep, right on the sidewalk in front of that luxury, high rise building, just off Wall Street.

I laugh now, shaking my head, just picturing the scene. What a crazy man. Just as I had fallen asleep on the casino floor in Las Vegas, on my 23rd birthday the year before, with my nice clothes on, I had fallen asleep on the sidewalk near Wall Street, exactly a year later.

It mattered not to me. The world is my home. I'm able to sleep anywhere that is the slightest of comfort.

Hours later, I awoke to sprinkles of water from the next door shop worker, hosing down the sidewalk. The morning sun shined as I opened my eyes from my deep sleep.

At first, I had forgotten where I was, and how I got there. And then the bitter memory of what had happened the night before came back to me.

I slowly stood up, dusted myself off, took a deep breath, and began to walk through New York City, on my way to the subway to return home.

That morning, I had become a new man! I knew that I was now definitely 24 years old! The previous night's events changed me. It made me realize, more than ever before, that I could not depend or put all my hopes on any one person ever again, even my brother.

I knew that the only One that I could fully, without a doubt, depend on, was the Lord Jesus Christ that resided inside me!

That morning, the world looked completely different than it had ever looked before, as I walked through the city with a face of solid stone. I had automatically become more focused. I had undergone the next phase of my divine transformation as I slept on that Financial District sidewalk. I had become a man!

I know now, that the Lord made me go through that experience, first, to make me realize what alcohol and lust can do to me if I wasn't careful. He also may have been protecting me from a great disaster. And I had no idea.

Secondly, the Lord made me go through that experience because I needed an unforgettable catalyst to propel me into the right direction that He wanted me to go in my new year of life! It was time for change in my life!

Chapter 23

One day, shortly after my 24th birthday, my brother asked me to do him a favor and wait behind in the basement of the luxury retail store in Soho that we called home, until a real estate broker and the potential buyer arrived.

I was to let them in, and allow them to inspect the building. Being an eternal optimist, I saw this as an opportunity to meet the broker and buyer and help them make a deal. I got dressed up, tidied up the place, and waited for them to arrive.

When they arrived, I greeted them with a smile, introduced myself, and began to make conversation with the potential buyer, the broker, and his beautiful fiancé.

They all seemed like great people, but on that warm, sunny day, I immediately had great chemistry with the Sicilian broker, Barnabas, and his fiancée, Claire.

I went out of my way to help them find a specific key that they needed to inspect the upstairs floors. I offered them refreshments. I treated them as if I were the owner of the building trying to make the sale of that $10,000,000 dollar plus property.

Before we parted ways, I exchanged contact information with Barnabas, the broker, as well as the potential Italian buyer.

I remember thinking to myself, "If I can help Barnabas, or the owner, who was my brother's client and friend, sell this building, then my financial dilemma would be a thing of the past."

The engine of my mind began to turn in motion once again! I could see the clear, endless possibilities!

When I was in Los Angeles, I had tried to broker a few multimillion dollar luxury mansions, so I had already learned a bit about selling real estate. This would be nothing new to me.

I lived with my brother for a few more days after meeting Barnabas. I networked with as many New Yorkers as possible, attempting to connect them with Barnabas.

Then later, I moved back to live with my parents in New Jersey. I had completely run out of money, and my brother just could not afford to have me there.

What was I going to do with my life? I needed some sort of income. Upon my return to New Jersey, my parents, with my best interest at heart, offered many suggestions about getting a regular job.

My dad tried to convince me to work at the airport with him. However, I refused to settle.

Not that there is anything wrong with working in the airport. If you love airports as I do, and that is your dream job, then by all means, go for it.

But with my wild, ambitious dreams, there was no way that I was going to commit to a long term job such as that. I was set on modeling, entertainment, athletics, finance, and real estate, just as I had always been for the majority of my adult life.

Day after day went by. Week after week went by. No good opportunity seemed to come my way. Soon, I felt helpless. I felt trapped.

I asked myself many times, "Why did I leave Los Angeles?"

I kept to myself in my parents' home for many days, trying to find the answers that I was searching for.

Then, I recall one night, sitting on the floor, alone in my sister's bedroom with the door closed. I had a hooded sweat shirt over my head. My face was tucked down between my knees.

I recall that night being one of the lowest moments of my life. I seemed to have all the answers my entire life. And now, I was blank, empty, with absolutely no solution.

For the first time in my life, I felt like, not necessarily dying, but I felt like disappearing! I did not want to be in that house. I did not want to be in that town. I did not want to be in that state. I just wanted my old life back, the days that it was easy to get money, the days that I lived in luxury. It had only been months since those days. However, sitting in that cold, lonely room, it felt like those great days were a lifetime ago!

I asked Jesus, "Please, help me! Help me find the answer...!"

Looking back, I can see my heavenly Father raise up from His thrown in Heaven, and begin to go to swift action!

For many days however, I could see nothing happening. I decided to humble myself. I took one of the suggestions of my family, which was to go to a company that finds people in my situation temporary work on a daily basis.

Most of the jobs would be manual labor. Most of the workers were struggling convicted felons and drug addicts. I swallowed my pride. I needed any form of money. I would be compensated about $50 dollars for a full day's work. It would have to do.

So, at about 4 A.M., every morning, I awoke, showered, put on some old working clothes and boots, and then made my way out of my parents' house. I had to catch a bus, a train, then walk about a quarter of a mile to the office in the dark, and then wait with a few dozen other workers, in hope that there would be jobs for us that day.

By the grace of God, there usually was. Throughout that time, I worked in a bakery and did dishes, cleaned, and mopped the floors all day.

Other times, I worked in a furniture store, taking out garbage, helping customers load their furniture into their vehicles, and doing other manual labor.

Other days, I worked in the mall, arranging products and moving heavy supplies. I would always return home extremely hungry and tired.

Some days, I had to walk miles, to and from the job location. My muscles ached. My feet hurt. But I never complained. As I worked, I cheerfully reminded myself that this is only temporary, and that good days are coming soon!

I made the best out of my situation. I always went to work with a positive attitude and a smile on my face. I worked diligently, despite the fact that this was not the work that I wanted to do.

I knew that God was testing and strengthening my faith and character during this transitional season.

My various employers loved and respected me. They spoke to me and treated me differently from the other workers. They could sense that there was something different about me. They all wanted me to stay and work for them permanently.

But I had other ideas! I was only passing through! I was truly inspired by the people that I worked with. As in jail, years back in Bloomington, Indiana, many confided with me, the problems that they were going through. They opened their hearts to me. I offered advice. I bonded with many of them. I realized that the Lord had not put me there to punish me, but to be inspired and to be an inspiration to many of those good people.

I was there to learn! I was there to give hope!

And just as it was, when I lived in the homeless shelter in Bloomington, Indiana, the vision was crystal clear in front of me.

In the mean time, I continued to keep in contact with Barnabas, the real estate broker, and continued to try to help broker some of the properties that he was attempting to sell.

I devoted a lot of my energy and time in attempt to close a deal with Barnabas. Many weeks went by.

Then finally, during one of our many telephone conversations, Barnabas, realizing my hard work and determination, and that I was serious about helping him close a deal, and not just another random person wasting his valuable time, asked me if I would like to work for the real estate firm that he worked for.

As I stood on the other end of the line, my heart rejoiced!

"That would be great!" I replied.

"I can't guarantee it, but I'll ask my boss if he would like to schedule an interview with you."

After I hung up the phone, I pumped my fist and praised the Lord with excitement! The Lord had told me in my heart prior, that if I work hard, and genuinely try to help Barnabas sell a building, that he would surely see my value, and have no choice but to offer me a job.

And now, the Lord's words were coming to pass! And I believe that the only reason that Barnabas offered me the job was because of trust!

Not just the fact that he trusted me, but the fact that, days prior, when he asked me if he could speak directly with my potential buyer for one of his $10,000,000 dollars plus buildings that he was attempting to sell, I was willing to trust him and set up a conference call between them.

Most people would advise that I never allow my potential buyer and another broker to speak directly and exchange information, that I should be the mediator between the two.

However, I trusted Christ, that I should trust Barnabas. And because of that simple trust, I was on the verge of being thrust into a greater direction! Trust, my friend, is the key!

Many days went by. I had not heard anything from Barnabas. I was tempted to get frustrated and lose hope and think that maybe, he was not serious about speaking to the owners of the company. But I chose to stay positive.

Then one day, I heard the house phone ringing. My mother answered. Moments later, I heard her call out my name.

"Maubrey... You have a phone call." she said.

I was not expecting any calls that day, so I wondered who it was. It was Barnabas! He told me the good news, that I was basically hired, and that I should come in for a briefing.

I still remember the feeling in my heart that afternoon. I was jubilant! I was happy to be able to work in New York City. I was happy to be given the opportunity to use my brain to make money.

And I wouldn't be working for just an average real estate company. The real estate company was one the top five commercial real estate firms in New York! They specialized in only selling big buildings, buildings selling for up to $100,000,000 dollars and more!

That was perfect for me! My plan was to sell a few buildings while continuing to pursue my modeling career, and then finally get back into training to become a professional athlete. I knew that this was the opportunity that I had been waiting and praying for.

I remember going in to the office for the briefing on the first day. My shoes were old and torn at the toes. The heels were worn at the corners. I could not afford to buy new shoes, but I refused to let that stop me from entering my blessing.

That first day, I recall getting out of the New York City subway, walking through 6th Avenue and making a left into 20th Street, walking happily until I reached the great office building.

From the moment I exited the elevator and walked into the waiting area and was greeted nicely by the secretary, I felt right at home. I knew that this was a place for me.

Barnabas later came with a big smile and hug to say hello to me. It seemed that he was almost as excited to have me part of the company as I was. He took me to a conference room to be briefed by Charlie, one of the managers of the firm. Charlie welcomed me warmly as well, and then briefed me about selling buildings.

Next, I was given a tour of the office and introduced to everyone. One by one, I said "Hi" and shook all the brokers' hands.

The company had a family atmosphere. A majority of the brokers were related, many of them Italian. I knew that I was going to fit right in! I was eager to learn from the best negotiators in the world!

Chapter 24

For the following few months, I devoted myself to real estate. I became engulfed! I did nothing but eat, sleep, and think real estate.

From Monday through Friday, I awoke at about 6 A.M. in the morning and was at work before 9 A.M.

Every morning, I got out of bed excited and enthusiastic about the day ahead. I loved the daily trip to the city. I felt as if I was accomplishing something each day. I loved the train rides, coming out of the subway into the streets of Manhattan, buying breakfast in the morning, and walking the remaining few blocks to the office.

Little by little, I was earning and saving money again. My old, worn clothes that I used to wear, turned into nice, fashionable clothes. As I learned daily, my confidence while speaking to building owners and potential buyers on the phone increased.

I soon developed great and lasting relationships with all of my partners. I loved them all, and respected them for their knowledge and wisdom.

From about 9 A.M. to 1 P.M., I dialed the phone nonstop, attempting to reach New York City building owners until my fingers hurt. I knew that real estate, like most businesses, was just a numbers game. The more I dialed, the better odds I would have of selling a building.

Then, when it was time for my lunch at 1 P.M., I would escape the fast paced office, to a secret world of my own. That one hour of lunch was my one moment of tranquility throughout the day.

I would usually go to a nice restaurant and have a peaceful, quiet meal. Oftentimes, I would bring travel magazines, cruise ship magazines, luxury hotel and resort magazines, as well as high fashion magazines to lunch and get lost in the pages, allowing my imagination to go wild, as I imagined myself vacationing in those exotic places and living that blessed life.

When my hour had passed, it was right back to work. I worked and worked until about 6 or 7 P.M. Some nights, I would stay well into the late hours of the night. I was determined! Nothing was going to stop me from reaching my final destination!

I knew that I had to keep my body in peak condition for my modeling and athletic career that I was slowly developing. I could not lose what God had given me, just because I was working in an office all day.

So within a few months, I got a membership with a high-end gym that was just two blocks away from the office. I knew that paying the extra price for a high-end gym membership would allow me to network with potential clients, while keeping me in a blissful state of mind.

I worked extremely hard all day in the office, then, no matter how exhausted I was, I would go straight to the gym after work.

Month after month went by. I was learning so much. It seemed that I was getting closer and closer to making my first deal. I became more engulfed in real estate.

And then one day, I received the email that I had been waiting and hoping for, for so long! It truly was a miracle!

An agent from one of the top ten modeling agencies in the nation had seen my photographs online, and asked me if I ever thought about modeling.

The modeling agent wanted me to come in to the office to see me in person. It was a bitter-sweet victory. I had no idea what to do.

I thought to myself, "If I begin to model full time, there is no guarantee that I would make enough money to survive."

Also, I felt that I was so close to selling a building. If I left now, it would feel like I had wasted so much time and energy.

I knew that my bosses would not allow me to miss even a day of work. I could easily be fired and replaced, despite my hard work ethic.

What a dilemma the Lord was testing me with. Should I risk hundreds of thousands of dollars of commission from selling a building? Or should I risk a once-in-a-lifetime opportunity to be represented by one of the top modeling agencies in the world?

What would you do...?

I sought counsel from a few friends and family members. I received different advice. I decided to hold back, and not reply to the modeling agent's email until I had made a decision.

After many days of considering all my options and praying over it, I made a decision!

I decided to move forward with real estate for the time being. My plan was to sell at least one building and then reply to the modeling agent's email.

I figured that if the modeling agency really wanted to represent me, then it wouldn't matter when I came to them. At least I would be financially secure with the money that I would make from selling a building.

I must admit that at the same time, in the back of my mind, I knew that there was a possibility that the offer may not still be there after a certain amount of time had gone by. But my decision was made. I had to stand by it!

Month after month, that email from the modeling agent remained unanswered. The seasons changed. Spring turned to summer. Summer turned to autumn. I had toured the insides of many multimillion dollar buildings in New York. I had met and negotiated with some of the most affluent clients in New York City.

Although it had been close to a year, and still, I was yet to sell a building, the Lord was blessing me in supernatural ways. My wisdom was expanding rapidly. I started businesses online. I was blessed with enough funds to start saving at least 20% of my income.

For the first time in my life, through reading the Bible, I began tithing to Joel Osteen Ministries. That is when the miracles and blessings increased in abundance!

I can never forget one night, a few months after I began to tithe. It was late at night, well past two in the morning. I sat there, all alone, in front of the computer in my dark room. I had just placed an order to buy thousands of shares of a stock online that I had just read about, minutes before, online. I had not too much information about the stock. I just had a good feeling. I really needed all the rest of the money in my bank account to pay expenses and buy basic necessities.

But the Lord was telling me in my heart to pay my tithe online, to Joel Osteen Ministries. I have to be honest, from the moment I clicked the link to pay the tithe, my chest burned. I knew that I needed that money. But I knew that I had done the right thing in serving Christ, and advancing the word of The Kingdom of Heaven!

I turned the computer off, crashed into my pillow, and then fell asleep, late that night. As I slept, my Father in Heaven began to move in a mighty way, because of my obedience!

The next day was astonishing! That stock that I had bought thousands of shares of, just before sending my tithe, had multiplied greatly!

A normal good day for a stock to increase would be around 5%. That would be good cause to celebrate. My stock did not increase 5%, 10%, or even 20%. It climbed over 50% during the very early hours of the morning! I was ecstatic as I tracked my stock on my iPhone in the office that day.

60%...80%...100%, my stock climbed! I could not contain my excitement! The majority of my partners in the office became aware of the news!

But the Lord Jesus was not done showing me the rewards of giving to His Kingdom! All throughout the remainder of that work day, the stock continued to climb! 150%...200%...

I recall my partners at work urging me to sell! I refused. I knew that the Lord was not done showing me His great power! The stock continued to skyrocket! 250%...275%... I could barely stay in my seat.

Finally, my stock had settled at around a 300% increase! I had never been in so much euphoria. I floated on cloud nine the entire day. My co-workers were absolutely amazed!

Once again, I had witnessed, firsthand, the glory of the Lord! Through my generosity, cheerful givings, and total trust in the direction of The Savior, I discovered a new gift! I discovered a new secret!

Another time, not too long after, I had been waiting months and months to get some photographs from a photographer of a photo shoot that I had done. I was tempted to get frustrated, however, I remained cheerfully persistent.

I would call and call the photographer, send email after email, text message after text message. But still, for many months, the photographer told me that he had not gotten the time to edit my photos.

Then finally, I decided to just stop contacting him. If the photographer wasn't willing to give me my photos, I would be at peace no matter what.

It had been nearly two months since my last contact with him. Then one fateful night, as I sat alone, in front of my computer, in my dark room, well past midnight, I debated again, whether to give an extra portion of donations to Joel Osteen Ministries online.

Once again, as before, I could really use all the money that I had. But the Lord was telling me deep down, that I should give! So, I gave. I then turned off the computer and went to bed.

As God is my witness, just as I closed my eyes to sleep, well past midnight, I received a sudden text message! My eyes reopened.

"Who in the world could be texting me at this time of the night?" I thought to myself.

I got out of the bed, looked at my phone, and was absolutely amazed at what I read!

"Come get your pictures..." the text read.

It was the photographer, who I had been attempting to get my pictures from, for all those months! My heart jumped! I knew that Christ had performed a miracle!

Because I had made a double donation to The Kingdom of Heaven, the Lord had blessed me with priceless photographs. He wanted to show me, so that there be no doubt, that He rewards His obedient children.

I can see the Lord in Heaven, patiently waiting to see if I would sow a double portion seed. I can see Him swiftly entering the body and mind of the photographer, taking over his conscience and subconscious, and causing him to text me.

The Lord will do amazing and astonishing things for you, if you only give cheerfully!

Just when I thought I had seen it all in life, then came the day that I almost lost my life!

I was almost finished reading the Bible. It had been a long journey since I started well over a year before. Along the way, I had learned about the powers of fasting through Christ Jesus.

One fateful day, I decided to fast and meditate on Jesus until sunset. It was a great and peaceful day for me. When the sun finally set that evening, I broke my fast with a light meal.

It was the weekend, so as usual, I was preparing to go out to The City that night to celebrate and network. My brother was with me. We celebrated all night with a Saudi Arabian prince and his entourage. It was a night to remember!

Drink after drink, the prince and my brother offered me. It was near my 25th birthday, so I was treated very well that night. There were lots of great music, beautiful, exotic women dancing, and champagne flowing continuously.

It wasn't before long that I became completely intoxicated. A few hours later, the Saudi prince, the entourage, my brother, and I were off to the next night club.

Again, more champagne began to pour in... More music, more celebration, more women!

As usual, later, I did my trademark wondering off from the group. I recall dancing with beautiful women, meeting new people, and having a wonderful time as I mingled in the nightclub.

By that point, I had more drinks in my system to last a week! Before I realized it, the nightclub was nearly cleared out with less than a dozen people in the club. I had no idea where time had gone.

The prince and my brother had disappeared. The music had been lowered. I remember sitting at one of the tables all alone thinking how great a night I had, but wondering where my party had went.

My brother's cell phone battery must have died, because I recall not being able to contact him. I decided, finally, that it was time to go home, back to my parents' house in New Jersey.

I began the long journey from the Meatpacking District of New York City. I blissfully floated to the subway to catch the first connecting train to the garden state. As usual, I fell asleep on the train, waking up just as the train arrived at the connecting train station in New Jersey.

Half asleep, I exited the train onto the platform, unaware that the next few moments would change my life!

As I waited on the platform for the connecting train to arrive, suddenly, I heard and felt the loudest slap on the right side of my face! I had never felt a stinging slap so hard!

What was it...? I had dozed off, collapsed and fell five feet down, face first, into the train tracks below!

I remember waking up, in slow motion. At first, I had no idea what had just happened. I had no idea where I was. I thought I was dreaming. It felt like a movie.

With the sting of my face slapping the train tracks still painfully vibrating in my head, I slowly opened my eyes and looked straight ahead. I remember seeing the head light of the train in the far distance. It must have been a mile away.

Still not realizing the severity of what had just happened, I slowly shook my head from left to right to clear my mind. I could hear screams and gasps from women and men in the background.

Slowly, I lifted myself to my feet, dusted myself off, and hoisted myself on top of the five foot platform.

Still dazed, I asked myself, "How did I end up in the train tracks?"

Onlookers stared at me as if they were looking at a ghost. I limped away from the edge of the platform.

Just as I began to regain my senses, I recall suddenly seeing an older man from my homeland of Ghana, standing by me, asking me if I was ok. He could tell that I was of Ghanaian decent as well. I bent down to attend my left leg, just below my knee. It was sore. Soon, I felt and saw blood running down my leg into my shoes.

"You fell asleep..." the Ghanaian man said solemnly.

He told of how he noticed me dozing off, seconds before falling head first into the tracks. I was shocked! I could not believe that I almost lost my life! It was a surreal and humbling moment for me.

Moments later, the train arrived. I boarded it and continued my journey home.

When I awoke later that day, what had happened sunk in. I realized how fortunate and blessed I was to still have my life.

Anything could have happened as a result of that fall. I could have broken bones. I could have lost some teeth. I could have broken my neck and become paralyzed. I could have severely cut and damaged my face. I could have died!

What if I would have fallen just a few minutes later, just as the train was arriving? Once more, my Father in Heaven had supernaturally wrapped His loving wings around me and shielded me with His divine protection.

How else could a person fall face first, five feet down into train tracks, without an injury, but a small cut below the knee? It is the power of Christ!

I wondered how I lost consciousness on the platform. I had drank far more in the past, but never collapsed before. I received a divine revelation later that day. I realized that there were many factors involved, prior to my collapse.

First, I remembered that I had been fasting all day. Second, I was running on virtually no sleep. And to add to those two factors, I was incredibly intoxicated!

Days later, I received another revelation as I journeyed on my chronological, daily readings of the Holy Bible. I suddenly stumbled upon the scriptures that spoke of alcohol.

The revelation was that it is not a sin to drink alcohol in moderation, but it is in fact a sin to become drunk with alcohol. It was truly an eye-opening, mind-blowing moment for me!

The Lord put those scriptures right in front of me, as clear as day, to show me that all His commandments and ways are to protect me from danger and death!

The commandments are to protect us from dying, if we would only obey them faithfully!

From that day onwards, I decided that from then on, if I were to drink, I would not drink to drunkenness again.

Day by day, the Lord was teaching me His ways, teaching me His divine wisdom!

I have told but a few people of that fateful night, not even my parents to this day. I could only imagine what people would think, especially my parents, if I had told them that their son had lost consciousness and fell head first into train tracks.

Chapter 25

Finally, the time had come! It was but a few days before my 25th birthday. I had been on this earth for an entire quarter century! I suddenly realized that I had just a few more pages of reading, before finishing reading the entire Holy Bible!

I pressed forward. I realized that if I continued reading at the pace that I was reading, then I could complete the Bible on my birthday!

What a journey through time it had been! For a year and a half, I had left the world and submerged myself into the greatest and holiest book of all time!

I had traveled through time, from the beginning, when God created the heavens and the earth, to the creation of Adam and Eve, to the first sins of man, to the story of Moses leading God's people from the bondages of slavery in Egypt to the land flowing with milk and honey in Israel, to the great stories of David and Goliath, and the great stories of King Solomon, to the murders, the lies, the wars, the sex, the good and the bad. I saw how the Lord always showed His infinite mercies to the ones who walked in righteousness and purity.

Time traveling through the pages of history, I witnessed Noah and his arch. I witnessed the first mention of Christ in the book of Isaiah. I witnessed the great prophets prophesying that one day soon, the Son of God would walk this earth.

The anticipation built for centuries.

Then finally, one fateful night in a small manger, Jesus, the only begotten Son of God arrived!!

I get chills running throughout my entire body as I imagine vivid images of that miraculous night in Bethlehem!

I read and witnessed how Christ, since childhood, performed many countless miracles for all who dared to ask and believe!

But some did not believe, despite endless signs and wonders. Some called Him a mere magician. Some even called Him evil. He was persecuted. He was despised. They saw that He was too powerful. They saw that He was too loved. They saw that He had too many powers.

So, as it was predestined, they killed Him, crucifying Him on the cross.

I continued through the Bible, the Book of Time, in my own secret, private world as the months passed by. I read about the tribulations of Paul, the former Jewish non believer, and persecutor of Christ, whose eyes were enlightened by the Lord, one awesome, fateful day!

I discovered the hidden secret, that from the moment Christ Jesus breathed His last breath of air on the cross, we won! The devil had been forever vanquished! Defeated, once and for all!

I became enlightened with the divine wisdom that all the troubles and worries of the world are simply clever, magical illusions by the devil, to keep the world in constant fear and confusion, and to cause us to live in doubt and uncertainty, wanting us to never fully, immovably believe in Jesus, the Son of God!

We have won, my friend! There are no "real" problems, if you have unshakable faith in The Christ! We have won!

At last, I had journeyed to the final book of Revelation. Then finally, just before the stroke of midnight, entering my 25th birthday, I completed the most amazing literary work of all time, the Holy Bible!

What a wonderful achievement that was for me! Instantly, I felt my mind, body and soul go to a new, higher dimension!

After a quarter of a century, my eyes were finally beginning to truly open! Like a new born baby tasting his first light. I felt an awesome sensation in my mind and body. It was at that very moment that I fully understood the meaning of being "born again"!

I had a sudden realization that the Lord purposely and perfectly architected every series of events over the previous year and a half, so that I may complete reading the Good Book on the day that His son was born!

I understood the significance of what had just transpired. It was truly my "birth day"! I was truly reborn on October 7, 2008!

The only way to even begin to comprehend the gravity of the story, and what I felt and experienced, is to read, chronologically, the entire Holy Bible, front to back, from Genesis to Revelation, in less than a year or two, with a believing, humble and open heart.

Not doing so would be akin to hearing stories about, or seeing only clips, trailers, and teasers of your absolute favorite movie of all time, and never being able to watch it for yourself!

Can you imagine not being able to experience the emotions and thrills of your all time favorite movie?

Those who have ears, let them hear my greatest advice! I can testify, more than a year after completing the Bible, and currently repeating the journey of reading it, until my days are gone, that it is this advice that will allow all your greatest and wildest dreams to seamlessly and miraculously come to fruition as mine are!

Those who have ears, let them hear!

I have unearthed the "Big Picture"!

The "Big Picture" is to keep Christ, the Son of God, first always, worshiping or seeking no other gods or idols, and to give and help…and give some more!

I had been gifted the greatest enlightenment! The blind fold had been removed from my eyes! The dark fog had been cleared! I boldly stepped into my new light, my new dimension! I understood who and what I was! I understood the reason that I was sent here! I understood the good that I was to do! I had been warned, groomed, and prepped for the enemy's attacks and temptations!

I searched my heart long and hard, took a good look at myself in the mirror, inhaled a deep breath, and accepted the calling!

I had a divine responsibility to the world. I would be held to a higher standard. I would be looked at with the greatest expectations. My life would never be the same from my 25th birthday!

The flame, of wanting to give more to the hungry, more to the naked, more to the helpless, and more to the orphans of the world, had been fanned! It was time to perfect my gifts!

At the same time period, the world was changing rapidly. America, in particular, was going through a renaissance of its own. We were on the brink of electing our first African American president, something that just two years prior, would be thought of, as impossible.

The global economy was in turmoil. Yet there seemed to be an unprecedented sense of hope and optimism in the air than ever before. Anticipation had built to its peak over the course of the previous two years. We were at the cusp of electing a great leader, that would guide not only the country, but the world into great prosperity!

It was such an inspiring time in history to be alive! A monumental miracle was about to unfold before the eyes of the entire world!

There were, however, many doubters, many naysayers, and many non believers. I recall walking through the streets of New York City early that morning, on my way to the real estate office to work on Election Day. How long the voting lines were! I could feel it in the air. History was about to be made on that crisp November day! Many people were about to become believers of the power of The Christ!

I remember sitting at home in the living room alone, later that night, in a black, leather, reclining chair. My parents and older brother were also glued to the live election count on the television in my parents' room. My younger sister, Samantha, was in university at the time.

There would be an eruption of cheer and celebration in our home each time the future president would win a state. The whole world, from Africa, to Russia, to China, to India, to Europe, and beyond was watching!

I received continued messages of rejoicing on my cell phone from all over the country, as the votes were tallied.

Then finally, after much anticipation and pandemonium, the news broke that sent shock waves of joy around the globe!

Barack Hussain Obama had become the first African American President of the United States of America! The world celebrated! It was a feeling of pure euphoria and hope!

I leaped into the air with joy and ran to the celebration in my parents' bedroom. We hugged, shouted with joy, and jumped with jubilation. It was an unforgettable feeling! We had just witnessed history!

Calls and messages exchanged to and from family members and friends from all over the world. I was in cloud nine! I felt as if I was the one who had just been elected leader of a great nation!

There was a strengthened sense of hope and confidence in my future. A young, brilliant boy of African descent had grown up and risen to become the leader of a great nation!

Christ had proved, yet again, that all things are possible for those who believe in Him!

Then, as high as I was with excitement, what happened just moments after, greatly shocked and devastated my world, bringing me abruptly down from my mental mountain top!

Minutes earlier, I had sent a text of celebration to Landon, one of my best friends from Indiana University.

"Have you heard about Carter?" he replied, referring to my former drug supplier and good friend that I looked up to and admired in Indiana.

The friend that, one day, I had got all dressed up in multiple layers of clothes to fight, years before in Bloomington.

"What happened to him?" I replied in a text message, a bit confused.

Meanwhile, my family was still celebrating in the background, as I sat on the burgundy carpet of their bedroom, waiting for a response from Landon.

Then came the reply that dropped my heart to the ground! "Carter is dead..." the devastating message from Landon read.

"He got shot in the head a few days ago."

Suddenly, a rage of pain, hurt, and anger filled my entire body! I paused for a second to digest the grave news. I had hoped that it was a cruel joke. But it wasn't. I startled my family and brought an abrupt silence to the room, as I released a great groan and spiked my phone containing Landon's message on the screen, onto the ground.

My parents' and brother's eyes quickly shifted to my direction.

"What's wrong!?" I heard my mother exclaim.

Trying my best to hold back tears, I stood up from the carpet, and stormed out of my parents' bedroom to be alone in my room. I cried so hard! Carter was a good guy. Despite his sins and illegal activities, he did not deserve to be murdered.

My family rushed into my bedroom to comfort me and to find out what troubled me.

I cried louder, as I struggled to let out the words to tell them what had happened to my old friend. My brother hugged and embraced me.

Once again, I had witnessed, first hand, the inevitable end result of drug dealing.

A gang, I later discovered from Landon, had invaded Carter's luxury Indianapolis home, demanding money and drugs from Carter's safe. Carter, not surprisingly, refused to cooperate and reveal the code to his safe.

I could remember a time, years back in Bloomington, when Carter joked about how he would never give robbers money or drugs if his home were ever to be invaded.

We would all cry in laughter as he described how he would use special super hero powers to blast the robbers away.

"Sonic-Boom!" he would yell jokingly, as the room burst into laughter.

That's the kind of guy Carter was, usually in a cheerful mood, usually ready to make someone laugh.

Because he refused to cooperate with the bandits, they shot him in the head! What a bitter-sweet night it was for me! Within a split second, I went from the highest mountain peak to the lowest valley.

I wished the Lord would have enlightened Carter, and saved him from the loosing life, as He had done to me, years prior. I wished he would have found a way out as I did.

I thought about the first time Landon took me to Carter's apartment to buy a bulk amount of ecstasy from him for the first time, during the first few weeks of sophomore year at Indiana University. I thought about how much in awe I was, at the tender age of 18 years old, of all his luxurious and expensive possessions. I thought about the time I had gotten all dressed up in multiple layers of clothes to fight him when he disrespected me on the phone. It was like going to fight my older brother.

I thought about how funny he was, how many times I would laugh every time I visited his home. I thought about how funny it was that he was always a bit paranoid of me, thinking that I may somehow be an undercover agent, working on him for years, and how I thought that about him as well. Carter had a good heart! He will certainly be missed and remembered by many!

Chapter 26

The sands of time continued to move forward. The chilling New York winter had arrived. I had been working for one of the top commercial real estate firms in New York for a year now.

Still, I had yet to sell a building. However, you would have not known, by the optimism, excitement, faith, and energy that I carried with me each and every day.

Everyone saw it as one of the darkest times in financial history. I thought they were crazy!

I, on the other hand, saw it as one of the greatest opportunities in history! I stayed in the office late hours, now faithfully and confidently attempting to broker buildings in Manhattan worth well over $100,000,000 dollars each. You could not convince me that it was impossible.

For many months, my superiors wanted me to try to sell cheaper buildings around $500,000 dollars to $1,000,000 dollars in Queens, Bronx, and Brooklyn.

They told me to just sell at least one building before attempting to sell half a billion dollar properties.

Again, I thought they were crazy! I knew that I could do anything through Christ! I believed in myself! I refused for much time, and then finally agreed to try to sell less expensive buildings for a few months in order to avoid being fired.

After compromising for a few months with no results, just as I had done when I decided to stop selling small amounts of drugs in Los Angeles, it was time for me to stop wasting time and shoot for the stars again!

This is who I am. This is who I've always been. This is who I'll always be! So once again, I pressed forward, putting no limits on the power of Christ!

At the same time, I was continuing to discover who I was, and working diligently to take my modeling and entertainment career to the next level!

During the Christmas holidays of 2008, a few months after I had completed reading the Holy Bible, the Lord deposited a double spoonful of compassion and love into my heart.

I founded The Maubrey Destined Foundation, a new and innovative non-profit Christian charitable organization, and began the journey of giving and helping to eradicate extreme poverty all around the world.

My dream is to completely eradicate extreme poverty, hunger, and disease in the world's poorest countries by building state-of-the-art schools and universities, hospitals and clinics, and churches and orphanages in the poorest locations in the world, through charitable donations from world leaders and generous people like you.

Schools and universities to educate, hospitals and clinics to prevent, treat, and cure illnesses and diseases, and churches and orphanages to give hope.

Early on, I believed that even if I did not get a donation or help from a single person, Christ would provide the funds and the strength to bring this, yet another ambitious, seemingly impossible dream to abundant fruition!

I had never been a writer, nor did I like writing the least bit. But Christ supernaturally gave me the words to write an online monthly letter of gratitude, encouragement, love, motivation, and inspiration to the group members of the foundation from all over the world. I felt a burning desire from Jesus to help those suffering the most!

Continuously, non-stop, wave after wave, great things just started to happen after I began and finished reading the Holy Bible! I had unlocked the vault of miracles and allowed them to come rushing into my life!

I began to do things that I never dreamed I would be able to do! I began to say things that I never had the boldness or confidence to say.

Long lost friends have tracked me down and united with me! I have gone places that I never dreamed I would be able to go! I've met the greatest and most wonderful people in the world! I've gained great wisdom! I've avoided bad decisions.

Chapter 27

VANESSA FIRE

Then came the day! The day that changed my life! The day that eventually led to the birth of this very book that you are reading at this moment!

It was but a few days after New Year's Day, 2009. For the first time, I had gotten the inspiration to do a photo shoot with a female model.

I had never shot with a female model before. So, sitting in front of the computer, alone in my bedroom that day, I diligently searched a popular modeling networking website for the perfect model.

I recall specifically searching for models that lived in Bronx, New York. I told myself that I wanted to work with a humble woman. I imagined that, if she lived in Bronx, the poorest borough in New York, then there was a good chance that she would be humble and down to earth.

I was believing to find a hidden treasure in the Bronx, a diamond in the rough!

After looking through hundreds and hundreds of photographs of different models, and not finding the look that I envisioned, I was tempted to give up and cease my search.

Then all of a sudden, I landed on the one photograph that changed my world! I became stuck, frozen in my seat! My heart skipped a beat! My heart melted! A sensational vibration shot throughout my entire body! I became week in the knees! Time stood perfectly still! I beheld an absolute work of art! A tall, slender princess!

What a beautiful queen! The purity and fire in her eyes, her long, dark lashes, her caramel skin, her plump, juicy lips, the mannequin-like pose that she was in, and her long, endless legs.

She posed in but a turquoise tank top and multicolored, polka-dot panties. I had become instantly enchanted by her beauty.

Then, my memory returned. I regained full consciousness. Suddenly, I recalled seeing that same photograph about a year before.

Why didn't I get this crippling feeling back then? Perhaps, subconsciously, I couldn't fathom her possibly being a real human being.

She was just too perfect in my eyes, too good to be true. Perhaps, my mind had not evolved yet.

Or, perhaps, Christ had not opened my eyes at the time.

You see, at this exact moment, you are literally surrounded by infinite treasures, but until you open your heart for Christ to open your eyes, you may never realize these treasures!

Those that have ears, let them hear!

I wanted to just step into the computer screen and sweep her off her feet, this beautiful Haitian girl from the Bronx. I wanted to be her hero. I wanted to be her prince! My search was over! She was the one!

But then, I had to take control of my emotions. I was not prepared, nor did I have a desire to fall in love at that time. I had to be honest but professional with her.

"I think you are beautiful." I told her in a message.
"Would you like to do a photo shoot together?"
Just moments later, to my complete surprise, I received a reply from her.
"Sure, why not?" I'll never forget her replying to me.

My heart could not help, but begin to race again!
"Hi Vanessa, what's your contact number? I'll be in the city tomorrow. I'd love to share our ideas over hot tea or coffee...xo Maubrey Destined" I replied.
I can't help but laugh now, as it is clear by my reply, that I had already fallen in love before even meeting this woman. I wonder what feelings went through her body after receiving a message from me.
"Vanessa Fire" this 20 year old woman's name was.
I had no idea, what type of adventurous journey Vanessa and I were about to embark on!
We exchanged numbers and then made arrangements to meet in New York City after I finish working out at the gym.
I remember Vanessa calling me the day of, asking me whether I thought it was best to reschedule our meeting for a more convenient date. I persuaded her to follow through and meet me that evening.
I was more than willing to adjust my schedule for her. I knew in my heart, that if we did not meet that night, that there was a great chance that we would never meet.
I recall speaking to her in the locker room of my gym, after my hour long workout. I learned that she lived, and would be coming from the Upper West Side of Manhattan. That was a surprise. She had recently moved from the Bronx.
Here I was, looking for a humble woman, far away from reach, and now, it seemed that Christ had given me a humble woman, closer to reach.
My anticipation climbed, knowing that I was but a few moments from meeting this princess!

Moments later, I walked through the cold winter streets of New York City, to our rendezvous point, just a few blocks from my gym.

For a few minutes, at the corner of 5th Avenue and 19th Street, I stood patiently at the busy New York City intersection. My heart jumped each and every time a woman who even remotely resembled Vanessa walked by.

And then she appeared! I'll never forget the moment that I first laid eyes on her! Those beautiful cat eyes! I stood in confidence, with a slight smile on my face, as she cat-walked gracefully across the street.

That walk, those black boots, those black pants, that black pea coat, that black scarf, and that black hat!

We seemed to smile at one another, as if we shared a secret, as if we knew that we were in for a long adventure together.

We kissed one another on the cheek and shared a warm hug. We talked as we walked, studying one another's faces.

"You look good…!" she said with a French, Creole accent as she looked into my eyes with a smile. "…I like you."

I smiled and returned the compliment. We wondered where to go for tea and to talk about our ideas for the photo shoot.

We finally decided on the food court of the nearby Whole Foods supermarket in Union Square. Anywhere, to get out of the frigid cold that night!

We entered Whole Foods Market, walked upstairs to the food court, and found the perfect place to sit. It was the only available table for two in the entire packed food court, as if God had reserved the table just for us. He certainly did, in absolute control of everything in our lives.

Already, things were just flowing perfectly for Vanessa and me! I ordered two extra large cups of hot tea for the both of us. We showed each other our portfolios and continued to converse.

As we sipped on our hot teas, we spoke a bit about fashion and our ideas for the photo shoot, but for the most part, we spoke about life, love, interests, and got to know each other.

We talked and talked and talked. I could listen to her sweet French, Creole accent for eternity! I melted in my seat. We were learning so much about one another.

For some reason, we were extremely open to each other. Being a very, very private person, I had never fully opened up to a woman. Not even with my past girlfriends.

However, the chemistry was extremely intense! More intense than I had ever felt in my life! Time had flown by before our eyes. Before Vanessa and I realized it, Whole Foods grocery store was closing!

You could see the stars through the large glass, floor to ceiling, viewing window of the food court. You could see the building lights and the Empire State Building lit up in the background.

The moon was out. The New York city lights filled the streets. The scene was absolutely majestic! Our barely touched hot cups of tea had turned room temperature. The once packed food court was now empty. We laughed, realizing that we were the last ones left. We had talked the night away!

I could not believe where the time had gone. I had planned on meeting Vanessa for only 30 minutes or so, an hour the most, to briefly discuss our ideas for the photo shoot, but had spent close to five whole hours talking!

Never in my life, had I had a deep, continuous conversation for more than an hour or two, with a woman, or any person, for that matter! It was incredible! I knew, in my heart, that this woman was something special!

As I walked Vanessa to the subway station, we laughed, as we kept bumping into one another, walking into one another's path. It seemed that love had completely taken away our senses of balance.

When we finally arrived at the subway station, where she was to catch her train back home, to the Upper West Side, I felt a bit sad. An amazing experience had come to a close.

We made plans to follow up with one another to do the shoot. We hugged and bid farewell to one another. I felt an unusually soothing warmth in her hug.

All through my journey back home to New Jersey, I thought of how amazing a woman Vanessa was. However, for some reason, I could not help but to think that there was a good possibility that I would not hear from her ever again.

At times, that is just the nature of life. That was surely far from the case. The very following evening, to my surprise, I received a call. It was Vanessa! My heart smiled. We spoke briefly about the project, but seemed to have drifted off into a deep conversation again.

One hour went by. Two hours went by. 3 hours...What was going on? What was the Lord up to, up there in the heavens? I could imagine Him laughing a hefty laugh on the thrown in Heaven.

Our conversations seemed to flow just so seamlessly. What an intense chemistry! It seemed like we had picked off right where we left off, from the night before. I had never heard of, only in fairy tale story books, or experienced anything like what was happening!

Well past midnight , having to wake up around six o'clock in the morning to go to work, I went to bed that night in pure euphoria!

After that second deep and long conversation, I was sure that she was falling for me as I was for her. There was no doubt!

The following morning, I went to work with a new joy in my heart. There was no hiding, that I had an awesome secret, that I had found another hidden treasure!

I imagined, like most of my past relationships, that it would be some days, or even weeks before Vanessa and I spoke on the phone again.

Once again, I was wrong. Without fail, my love, each and every night, following our first acquaintance in Whole Foods, would call me a little after 9 P.M.

It was quite unbelievable! No one had ever shown me that much love and attention before. She made me feel special. She made me feel wanted.

Some nights, I thought that she would tire from calling me. But she never did. The more we spoke on the phone, the closer our souls came. I realized that my princess had fallen in love with me!

In the very beginning, I promised myself that I would not allow our relationship to escalate past friendship, at least not after many months, or even years, after getting to know her. I wanted to have a beautiful woman, as just a friend, for once in my life.

I had finished reading the Holy Bible just months prior, so I had premeditated to not let our nightly telephone conversations turn sexual. I did not want to have to test my will power.

After a few nights of deep conversations on the phone, my love started to seduce me. I tried my best to fight it.

At first, every time Vanessa would steer our conversation sexual, I would be able to cleverly change the subject. We laughed, as she pointed out my will power.

"Oh, so you're playing hard to get…" I remember her suddenly saying with her sweet French accent.

She had never experienced anything like it. At that point, we were both fully aware that we were physically and sexually attracted to one another.

Another night, she would tell me that she wanted me to be her personal trainer, to help her improve her virtually perfect body. I laughed in my head. I knew exactly what she was up to.

Moments later, she would send photographs of her, wearing sexy lingerie to my email. She would whisper in my ear what she would do to me in bed, how she would kiss and caress me, and how good we could make each other feel.

This woman was persistent!

"I know what you are doing to me." I would say playfully on the phone.

She would laugh mischievously, acting as if she had no idea what I was talking about.

Alas, I had fallen to temptation. I had been seduced by this 20 year old woman! And after less than two weeks of continuous, nightly conversations, I had agreed to come to her apartment in the Upper West Side of New York to make love to her.

I was obviously not as strong willed about sex with beautiful women as I thought I was. Or perhaps, it was because I saw Fire as "the one".

We met at a restaurant to get a quick bite to eat, then, holding hands, we strolled a few blocks to her apartment.

She was renting a room in the apartment of an older Spanish woman. She introduced me as her boyfriend.

While in Vanessa's room, we made small talk, both of us obviously a bit nervous about what was about to happen. I felt butterflies in my chest the entire time. Then there was silence in the bedroom.

Finally, our big, soft lips began to kiss. I could taste her mouth moisten with cool saliva, as our passionate kisses intensified. It was like kissing an angel for the first time!

I glided my palms up the sides of her lovely face. We began to undress one another. I caressed her breasts. We entered the bed. I laid on my back. She climbed on top of me. We kissed passionately.

Then, I slowly entered inside her. I could feel her warmth and moistness. She moaned with every inch. Making love to Vanessa was the greatest sensation that I had ever felt up to that moment!

I had waited so long. I had been so patient. I had saved myself for such a long time. This bronze princess was well worth the year and a half wait for sex!

I became one with her with every stroke. I could see the pain and pleasure in her sweaty face. Our spirits were forever connected! I had found my last love!

After that unforgettable night together, again, I imagined that, that may have been the last time that I would ever see the beautiful Vanessa Fire. I thought something like that, something that strong, something that potent, was just too good to be true!

Wrong again. Without fail, her nightly calls continued to pour in, evening after evening, week after week.

We were traveling to a different dimension together, a dimension that neither of us had ever been before!

Words on this page could not come close to describing what was happening to us! I would think of Vanessa when I awoke in the morning. I would think of Vanessa all day at the office. And when I returned home from work at night, we would talk on the phone deep, past the midnight hours.

Our hearts yearned for one another all through the week. It burned, not to be together every waking moment. I comforted Vanessa on the phone. I let her know how much I loved her.

Then, during the weekends, we were inseparable. I would journey, traveling long distances, from my home in New Jersey, to the Upper West Side of Manhattan to see her.

I would walk a quarter mile from my home to the bus stop. I would take the bus to the main shopping center in the bordering town. I would exit the bus and would walk another quarter mile to the train station. After taking the first train, I would transfer to another train headed to New York City. When I arrived in New York City, I would exit the subway, into the busy streets of New York City to catch a third train.

Finally, after arriving at Vanessa's stop in the Upper West Side, I would trek another quarter mile to my beloved's apartment building.

I would always get the greatest feeling in my heart whenever I would enter her apartment complex, knowing that I was but a few moments from seeing my princess!

We would spend the entire weekend together, most times, never even leaving her apartment! In her room all day, we would make sweet love, stare into each other's eyes, cuddle in bed, give each other massages, watch movies, and talk about pure nothingness.

It was perfect!

Before we knew it, the weekend had flown by! Only great love could make the sands of time fly so quickly. Only great love, indeed!

Chapter 28

Meanwhile, back in the office, during the work week, I persisted in my diligence to sell my first building. However, it seemed that it was time for the Lord to move me, yet again, into another direction.

Following the Christmas holidays, upon returning to work, we learned that there would be no more weekly pay for the handful of us new brokers, who had been getting weekly compensation for the past year.

The news was quite a shocker for most of us. Some brokers left immediately after hearing the news. Some waited a week to be certain. I had a hard decision to make. Should I stay at the firm and believe that I would close a deal before I ran out of the little money that I had saved over the course of the year? Or should I leave and pursue a different direction?

After careful consideration, I decided to stay with the firm for as long as I could afford to. I worked more diligently than ever. I increased my faith. However, I realize that when Jesus wants to push you into a higher level, it will be absolutely clear and obvious to you. You must allow Him to elevate you. You must allow Him to perform His miracles, despite not fully understanding how it would be possible. We must trust in the clear signs of the Lord!

A little over a month after working with no pay, living on my savings and stocks, I graciously decided to step down from my day-to-day office duties. The time had come for me to move forward!

I was surely sad to have to leave the people that I had come to love! Nevertheless, I had no regrets. Half of the office had left. The once busy and vibrant office was now a quiet and somber atmosphere.

How I would dearly miss these amazing people that I had come to love! From the secretaries to the owners, who had become family to me, the many laughs that were had in that office, the teamwork and camaraderie, the early morning meetings, and the great food that was shared daily throughout the work day.

I would miss the excitement of seeing a partner close a big deal, the coffee breaks, the building tours, the holiday gatherings and dinners, and the after work drinks. I would miss it all!

I had never seen anything like this. We truly were one big happy family. I started out at the complete end of the office, but within months, my work ethic, focus, and fire had landed me right next to the owners of the top commercial real estate firm in New York, and the country!

I had learned so much about business and life that year. What an amazing experience! It was like being paid to attend Harvard University. Perhaps, I did, after all, get that scholarship that I wanted!

After leaving the company, Christ went straight to work on my behalf! I suddenly received a blast of heavenly creativity, a sense of freedom, and clarity in my mind that I had never felt before!

My heart flooded with excitement! I saw the world in a new and refreshed light! I realized that I had been working in the office, focused on absolutely nothing but real estate for so long, that my creativity, innovativeness, and wild dreams had been suppressed.

Now, I was out of that matrix that I had created for the past year. The new Maubrey had emerged! The complex engine of my brain had been dusted off, well-oiled, and reactivated! I began to dream big again! My confidence in my future was multiplied!

Right from my bedroom of my parents' home, I started online businesses again. I stayed diversified. I kept in touch with all the bankers, buyers, and sellers that I had developed a good relationship with, over the course of the year.

I did not have much money, but I started to search diligently for real estate to invest in. I had learned too much, not to do so. Many friends and family members sought my advice and consultation in regards to finance, investing and real estate.

It was clear, after just a few moments of speaking with me, that I had a vast wealth of knowledge.

It is clear now, that the Lord sent me to that firm, not to sell billions of dollars worth of other peoples' buildings, but to prepare me for much greater deeds in the future. And the future is now!

I had spent all that time and effort, trying to sell billions of dollars of other peoples' buildings, then one day, weeks after leaving the firm, the Lord gave me the divine revelation!

It dawned on me! I realized something amazing! "I" am that billion dollar building that I had been trying to sell all along! "I" am that billion dollar product! "I" am that trillion dollar invention!

It's in your words. It's in your body! It's in your brain! It's in your hands! It's in your fingertips! Friend, no matter how bleak our circumstances may seem, we are all billion dollar packages, priceless, as a matter of fact!

We need only ask Christ daily, for the wisdom to realize precisely how to unlock our vault of infinite treasures. As we humbly ask Christ the Lord, the answers will be revealed continuously!

The seasons changed. Winter turned to spring. Fire's and my love had intensified to levels that I never knew existed. She was my fire storm, my blue lagoon. The more we got to know each other, the more alike we realized we were.

We were both passionate, both stubborn and hard headed, and both fierce! However, with all that we had in common, there were certain things that we strongly disagreed on.

I remember our first fight. We were in her bedroom. I listened as she spoke for quite a while about how a friend of hers had a foundation targeted on how African Americans are always treated unfairly, and how the country was set up so that we would not succeed.

After listening to her go on for some time, I had to interrupt. To me, it felt like that was just an excuse to live in mediocrity, especially with the experiences that I had overcome in my life as an African American.

I told her that I disagreed, pointing out the many African Americans who had thrived, especially, our first African American president, Barack Obama. I thought I could not give a better example than him. However, I could see the frustration and temperature rising in her face as I continued to speak. I could see her temper about to erupt.

However me, being opinionated and strong willed, as I've always been, I continued.

"If that is the case," I said, "Then, fair enough. But why not talk about the solution, and how to solve the problem, instead of complaining and gossiping about it continuously?"

Now, if you know any strong willed woman with the slightest of a temper, then you know that I had pushed the wrong button with that remark. There was a brief silence in the bedroom, suddenly, I could see her eyes ignite with furry.

She smashed the plate that she had in her hand on the floor, shattering it into a million pieces! My heart jumped! This was the first time I saw my princess lose her temper. I remained calm on the outside, but inside, I couldn't help but to be nervous.

"You know what?" she said, "I can't do this anymore!" implying that she wanted to break up with me.

My heart, for a moment, skipped a beat. But then, I remained calm. I knew that she could not possibly mean what she had just said. We had been through so much in so little time. We were far too deeply wrapped in the web of love, for her to mean what she said.

Had it not been true love, I would have left the moment the plate hit the floor. But she was my princess. I sat there quietly, as she continued to raise her voice and yell at me, getting everything that she had to say off her chest.

When Fire calmed down, I humbly apologized for the manner that I communicated my opinion to her.

Our love, as hard as it is to imagine, seemed to magnify even more after that first fight. There seemed to be no way of breaking our bond! We were two dragons, madly in love! With every disagreement, came a more potent love.

Once, after a disagreement, walking down the streets of the Upper West Side together, my fiery dove stormed away from me, once again telling me that it was over.

Again, with any other woman in my past, I would have let her go. As she stormed away, I thought briefly, whether or not to let her walk away. But love had me. I could not.

After a while of contemplating, I ran to her, apologized for the way what I told her came out, and then walked with her for blocks until she had calmed down.

Minutes later, we were holding hands. I loved this woman. And she loved me. There was nothing either of us could do about it!

Time passed by. Our love seemed to multiply with every kiss, with every breath. Then, yet again, in the subway station in Manhattan, just a few blocks away from her home, my fiery princess stormed away from me because I did not want to talk about her inviting a former love interest to stay in her apartment.

I stood there alone, watching her back as she stormed away. I felt so disrespected. I felt so insulted. I did not deserve to keep being treated that way.

In the past, this kind of fight and make-up relationship would be exciting for me. I would actually initiate it. But I was a new man now. I knew that in the end, it was not a healthy way to live with the love of your life.

I decided right there in the subway station, after about three months of being hopelessly in love with Fire, that I had to end our relationship.

After I exited the subway station, I immediately sent her a text message that I could not do this anymore. I knew that it would hurt her deeply, but I wanted her to feel the hurt that she made me feel. In my mind, this love story was over!

Many days went by. I could hardly eat. I could hardly sleep. I could hardly focus. My heart burned. I could feel her heart burning all the way across the Hudson River, from New Jersey.

I was tempted many days to pick up the phone and call her. I could do nothing to keep this mountain of a woman out of my thoughts! Every song brought her image to my conscience. Weeks went by. I suffered much without my love!

Then finally, late one evening, after weeks of agony and separation, I picked up the phone and dialed the numbers to connect to my heart, my love, my deep ocean!

"Hi..." I said somberly.

The moment Fire heard the sound of my voice, she began to weep. I could feel her intense sorrow and love through the phone. She had been waiting for so long, believing for so long, hoping that her prince would return.

Her prince was back! It pained just too much to live without my princess, not hearing the sound of her sweet, angelic voice nightly, not receiving her sweet text messages throughout the day, not sharing the laughs, the emotions, and the happiness.

That night of rekindled fire took our divine love to a whole new dimension. It seemed that we would last forever and ever! It seemed that our flame would burn for all eternity – that our love would stand the test of time!

Then, in the spring of 2009, our love would be tested yet again. For the first time, Fire and I would be separated by great time and distance.

Moving forward in my modeling and entertainment career, I had scheduled a handful of photo-shoots with various noted photographers in Los Angeles.

After almost two whole years away, I was returning to the heavenly land that I loved so dearly, the land that I abruptly left behind. But this time, I was returning a changed man! I was returning a brand new, wiser man!

I so wished that I could take my love with me for the two week stay. But I couldn't. In order to proceed with my dream, I had to leave my love behind. We cuddled and held each other so tightly together in the bed of her room preceding my departure, as if I were never returning.

Both of us knowing my unpredictable and spontaneous life, we feared that that was not at all unlikely.

And with a blink of an eye, I was on a flight to Los Angeles, California! If Fire and I thought we loved one another immensely, then our separation proved that we were absolutely, hopelessly in love!

Those two weeks away from Fire in Los Angeles were one of the hardest weeks of my entire life. It was very difficult, but we spoke on the phone each day. She would send me lovely photographs of her to keep my spirits up. Our hearts burned, how much we missed one another. But this time, I was not bus and train rides away.

I recall taking long walks through the beautiful Beverly Hills, talking to her on the phone. I would vividly describe the dazzling places that my eyes were witnessing. I wanted to make her feel that she was right there with me, holding my hand and staring into my almond eyes. We would talk and talk until my battery went low. It felt good to know that I had a good woman waiting for me back home.

With each conversation, I loved Fire more and more. I wished that I could reach into the phone and kiss her soft, sweet lips.

She told of how she did not think that I would actually leave. Perhaps, she got a sudden realization of how our future could be. I was a man always moving forward, likely to part from her at a moment's notice.

But I saw that as only temporary. I envisioned and dreamed of us traveling the globe together in the near future.

But was she willing to wait?

Chapter 29

Upon my return to the east coast, things slowly began to change. Although we loved one another with an eternal fire, it seemed that our differences began to outweigh our love.

Still, there were some topics that we just could not see eye to eye on. We realized that we saw the world in completely different ways.

I saw the world in a positive light, filled with infinite opportunities and miracles, despite the natural circumstances.

She, on the other hand, saw the world as the way it was. It seemed that our life experiences had led us down paths of different beliefs.

Nevertheless, I was willing to be patient. I was willing to wait. I was willing to trust God!

However, my darling princess was not. I remember the day that we finally broke up. Both of us, alone in her bedroom one morning, she became upset with me for something minor that I had done or said.

As she sat in the chair, grooming herself in front of the mirror, I tried my hardest, for the next few minutes to cheer her up, apologizing, hugging her, showering her with soft kisses, and showing my affection. But my sincere attempts to put a smile on her face failed.

I finally gave up and laid on her bed. I stared at the ceiling, beginning to seriously think about our relationship, and whether or not I could continue in the direction that we were going.

I realized that no longer could I effortlessly put a smile on my angel's face when she became upset. I loved Fire with all my heart, but I was not happy.

Minutes later, after she finished prepping herself in front of the mirror, finally she began to speak to me.

"Do you want to get something to eat?" she asked me.

I remained silent.

She asked again.

Still, I did not answer. I could see her becoming frustrated. I wanted her to know how I felt, just minutes before. I wanted her to know how hurt I was, so that perhaps, she would not treat me the way she did in the future.

I hoped that she would come to the bed, where I lay, and comfort me, hug me, apologize for how she overreacted, and shower me with sweet kisses as I had just done.

I wanted Fire's love. I wanted Fire's affection. However, what she gave me moments after was the complete opposite.

"You know what...? It's over...!" she exclaimed, "I'm not going to do this anymore!"

She asked me to leave. My heart dropped!

But then, I thought that perhaps, she did not mean what she had just said. I laid quietly on her bed, giving her a chance to cool down.

"I'm serious!" she said, looking me directly in the eye.

I had never seen that look from my love before. It was at that moment, that I realized that she was serious. I had lost my love! She later entered the bed with me, her mind set that it was over, and that I would be out of her life within a few moments.

In the bed together, I attempted to hold her hand. She shoved me away. I attempted to hold her body. Again, I was shoved away. Her heart was a glacier!

"Just go…!" she told me.

"Just go!"

Those two simple words pierced like a dagger through my heart. Our five month story book love affair flashed before my eyes! My heart and soul burned like never before.

I felt like crying, but tears did not come out. I felt like shouting as loud as I could, but there was no sound in my voice. I felt betrayed, but there was nothing I could do about it.

Finally, after a moment of silence, with the palm of my right hand, I slapped the bed with all my might.

"That's f**ked up!" I exclaimed, "That's f**ked up!"

I could tell that I startled Fire. I don't believe that she had ever seen me lose my calm. I had not been that frustrated in a very long time.

It was truly over, and I knew it. My broken heart continued to burn! I got out of her bed, rushed to put my clothes on as fast as possible, wanting to get as far away from Fire as fast as possible, yet at the same time, hoping that a miracle would happen, and that she would tell me that she did not mean what she said.

But she never did.

But perhaps, a miracle did happen indeed. Perhaps, the miracle was the divine revelations that would follow our separation. I stormed out of Fire's apartment, down the staircase, and out of the building. I was absolutely steaming inside!

The sun beamed on my face. The world looked completely different this time. For the first time, I was leaving that apartment building, no longer with the love of Vanessa.

There are no words to describe the excruciating pain that my soul felt that afternoon! My mind was numb! My face was solid stone! I grinded my teeth! My jaws were locked! I had given this woman all my love. I had told her all my deepest secrets. I had lowered my defenses. I had entrusted her with my most guarded treasure, my heart!

And now, she had broken it into a billion pieces!

"How could she?" I thought.

"How can I go on without the woman that I love more than anyone or anything in the world?"

Chapter 30

SONG OF MAUBREY

Vanessa Fire was my everything! I saw her as the goddess that she was! I was ready to spend the rest of my life with her. I was willing to take her hand in marriage. I envisioned a great and spectacular celebration, as I unveiled her in her long, white wedding dress on our wedding day, making her my queen! I could see her sitting on the throne by my side.

I envisioned Fire drenched in sweat, squeezing my hand tightly, surrounded by doctors, her face glowing like the sun, screaming at the top of her lungs as she pushed out our first baby. I envisioned me showering her face with infinite kisses, as she gently held our baby in her arms.

I could see the bashful look in her eyes that she would give me when I used to speak sweet nothings to her.

I envisioned us living in big homes all around the world. I saw Fire and me growing old together, living a happy and abundant life.

Through my faithful eyes, I saw us spending eternity traveling through space and time together. I could see her face in the midnight stars! She was my love cruise. Her kisses were like the sweetest fruit. She made my heart soar across the sky! She brought a twinkle to my eyes. She was the rainbow to my storm. She was my blue lagoon. She was my tropical forest.

Her voice was like honey. Her touch was fine silk. She made my mind run wild. She was the frost atop my mountain, my sunrise and my sunset.

For eternity, I could write a thousand books, recite a thousand poems, and sing a thousand songs, about but one day with Vanessa Fire. She was my love's divine!

Chapter 31

THE MOTIVATION – IT IS TIME!

We made unsuccessful attempts to reunite again after that day. There were many factors that eventually led to the end of our love story.

She said she needed to love herself, before she could love me. She said she did not want to hold me back from my destiny.

But in the end, the best way that I can explain the cause of the end to my greatest love affair, is that: Our hearts were in sync, however, our minds, and views about life were not quite in sync.

Days later, as I sat idly on my bed, staring at my white bedroom wall, wondering what my future would hold, from the throne of Heaven, Christ, once again, entered me! I was given a revelation!

I picked up a pen...! I picked up a paper...! And writing, I began!

The revelation was that the Lord purposely and specifically brought this great woman into my life, that I may bring this great story to you!

I had to feel the greatest pain, in order to give the greatest book!

If you only believe, Jesus, the Lord, will use your pains, every one of them, and turn them into astonishing victories and blessings!

He said, "I have a great gift for you Maubrey, My son!"

"It is a book by you, to share with the world, but you don't have to worry about how you are going to write it! I, your Lord Jesus, will write it for you! I only need your body, your hands, and your willingness to do so! I will use you My son, to do this and many more great works, because of your indestructible, unshakable belief in Me!"

Unbeknownst to you, as you have read, the Lord Jesus Christ has used this book to hypnotize you! Hypnotize you to love deeply! Hypnotize you for wealth! Hypnotize you for greatness! Hypnotize you for abundance! Hypnotize you for unexplainable miracles from this point on that will boggle your mind!

And it can never be reversed! You shall always be blessed! You will have many trials, tests, tribulations, and adversities along the way, but never again, shall you fail to seamlessly conquer them all! Never again, shall you fail, in the name of Jesus Christ!

Don't believe me? Then don't take my word for it. See for yourself. Watch carefully, and observe the series of events that transpire from this moment on, and marvel at the unexplainable, indescribable wonders that begin to take place in your life!

It is not by chance, nor by coincidence that you are reading this book at this very moment in time! Take a moment... Look around! You are transformed!

This is a reinvention of the mind!

No longer are you of man, but of Christ, you are! No longer will you have fear! No longer will you have worry!

In the divine name of Jesus Christ of Nazareth, I break the spell of defeat! I break the spell of lack! I break the spell of poverty – financial and emotional! I break the spell of worry! I break the spell of depression! I break the spell of fear! I break the spell of addiction! I break the spell of anger!

I break the spell of hate! I break the spell of imbalance! I break the spell of gluttony! I break the spell of greed! I break the spell of lies! I break the spell of doubt! And I break the spell of uncertainty that you have been in your entire life!

I cancel the curse! I cancel the illusion! I disintegrate the smoke and dark clouds in front of your eyes! I awaken you now! In the potent name of Jesus!

I have gone through all my savings over the past year and a half, to bring this powerful, divine book of hope and inspiration to you. I have gone hungry. I have sacrificed my wants and desires. I have isolated myself. I have left this world, that you may be once and for all, confidently convinced, through my many trails, tribulations, long sufferings, and victories, about the almighty, indestructible power and compassion of our Lord, the Son of God – Jesus Christ!

Some in the past have helped me because I am a good person. Some may have helped me because they thought of themselves as good people. Others may have helped me because they thought that I had something to offer. Others may have helped me in order to use me in the future.

But it was the Holy Spirit of the Lord that entered and softened their hearts, that allowed and caused them to help me along my journey.

Every day, the Lord is thinking of new ways to astonish, impress, and baffle your mind with His miraculous wonders!

I will defy every and all theories of physics, science, philosophy, religion and evolution! And in the end, all that will remain is the word of Jesus – the word of God!

YOU, my friend, will defy every and all theories of physics. You will defy every and all theories of science. You will defy every and all theories of philosophy. You will defy every and all theories of religion. You will defy every and all theories of evolution!

You! You! You!

All your greatest dreams will come to bountiful and overflowing fruition! And in the end, all that will remain, standing strong, is the word of Jesus Christ, the one and only true Son of God!

It is Time!

Chapter 32

MY MISSION

My mission on Earth is quite clear.

I came and stayed in New York to become a man
I came to become a United States citizen
I came to learn from my older brother the areas I was lacking
I came to teach my older brother to become more pure
I came to be with my parents who I had been away from for 7
years
I came to encourage and guide my mom to pass the test to become
a Registered Nurse
I came to help and inspire my parents to become healthier and
start working out

I came to encourage my younger sister to follow her dreams, live healthily, and be a good older brother to her

I came to be in the early stages of my little niece's and nephew's lives and to be a positive memory in the future

I came to learn to become the greatest athlete

I came to learn how to become a top model

I came to learn to be the greatest entertainer

I came to understand and become comfortable in my skin

I came to humble myself

I came to relive my past, so that I could know my future

I came to share all the knowledge, differences, and wisdom that I had learned through my travels over the past 7 years

I came to rebuild and start from scratch

I came to make new lifelong friends

I came to get out of the matrix and into reality for a while

I came to prepare to take on the world

I came to learn and embrace my African roots through my family

I came to learn from the best in the world

I came to build my brand

I came to be inspired

I came to be enlightened

I came to purify my heart

I came to help

I came to give

I came to follow my true dreams

But most of all...

I came to inspire!

I met the love of my life

I lost the love of my life

My time is now up...

My job here is done!

It is time to go back to the future!

The Maubrey Destined Effect

Chapter 33

REVELATION

The journey to the Kingdom of Heaven is far from a perfect and sinless walk. It is about seeing a unicorn for the first time, in the middle of the long, lonely road, and having to decide whether to kill it, eat it, run away from it, or befriend it.

Each wise and righteous decision gets us closer to the Gates!

I have come from the land of Germany. I was sent to Ghana, and then, to the United States. I was raised in a poor and humble family. I have encountered many adversities. I have had many triumphs through Christ. I have always dreamt big! I have traveled the world. I have had great lovers.

I have committed many sins. I have lied. I have stolen. I have fornicated. I have committed adultery. I have been greedy. I have been selfish. I have been jailed. I have been homeless. I have been rich. I have been poor.

I have dealt about a half a million dollars in drugs. I have lived in exotic locales. I have driven fancy cars. Then I lost it all.

I was at the lowest point in my life. Then I found the Holy Bible.

I became transformed! I became born again! I have gained the greatest wisdom. I have gained the greatest knowledge. I have witnessed great miracles.

I have given up lies, both large and small. I have given up profanity. I have given up drunkenness. I have been freed of the spirit of lust. I have given up sex until I find my true queen. And if I should ever fall, like a phoenix out of the ashes, I shall rise again!

I have been enlightened by Jesus Christ. My future has been revealed!

I WILL raise the dead with my presence, my voice, my scent, and my touch
I WILL heal the sick
I WILL self-heal
I WILL comfort the needy
I WILL cast out demons
I WILL bless many
I WILL fly
I WILL teleport
I WILL lead many nations
I WILL travel the world
I WILL travel through space
I WILL travel through time
I WILL have telekinesis
I WILL have photographic memory
I WILL have telepathy
I WILL become the greatest athlete
I WILL move mountains
I WILL walk on water
I WILL become the richest man alive, and
I WILL give unlimited, infinite amounts away to the poor, the hungry and the orphaned
I WILL have supernatural, divine, and infinite wisdom
I WILL have supernatural, divine, and infinite knowledge
I WILL have supernatural, divine, and infinite understanding
I WILL create masterpiece music and art
I WILL have eternal life
I WILL have divine inventions, divine innovations, and divine epiphanies
I WILL touch and inspire many lives

"How!?" you ask.

The same way that I have experienced all the many magnificent miracles and wonders in my life. Through Jesus Christ, the Son of God!

By the time you are reading this, it has already begun!

Christ clearly said, "Verily, verily, I say unto you, He that believeth on Me, the works that I do shall he do also; and greater works than these shall he do; because I go unto My Father. And whatsoever ye shall ask in My name, that will I do, that the Father may be glorified in the Son. If ye shall ask any thing in my name, I will do it." John 14:12-14.

Those that have ears, let them hear.

You have now received the greatest wisdom.

Now, in Jesus' name, I ask that you do not keep this blessing to yourself, but share it with all that you see and meet from this moment on, for every seed that you plant will yield a bountiful harvest, stretching through eternity!

I bless you with the divine confidence and power in your words and actions, from this moment on!

The Lord said to me, "I shall make you ruler of many nations; more than the grains of sand on the earth!"

His promises are for you also! There are many other hidden worlds! There are many other secret dimensions!

As you steadfastly continue to give, and worship no other gods or idols on your journey to The Kingdom of Heaven, all the marvelous secrets will surely be revealed!

And so that there be no doubt as to whether my words have been figurative or literal, let it be known, that I speak in both literal and figurative realms!

Make no mistake…

I AM not Moses
I AM not Paul
I AM not David
I AM not Solomon
I AM not Jesus
I AM not God
I AM MAUBREY
I AM DESTINED
I AM Maubrey Destined!

The Maubrey Destined Effect

The Maubrey Destined *Effect*

TO BE
CONTINUED...

Special Thank You

First and foremost, I'd like to give thanks to the Lord and Savior, Jesus Christ for all that He has done for me and continues to do in my life. I'd also like to thank everyone who believed in me from the beginning. I thank everyone who has supported me from the beginning. I thank everyone who has encouraged me. Thank you all from the very bottom of my heart!

Sincerely,
Maubrey Destined

For *Exclusive* Photos, Videos

&

More Healing

Visit

http://www.maubreydestined.com

Add Me

http://www.facebook.com/maubrey

To:

James

This is

your

time!

S2Ho

6/16/14

The Maubrey Destined Effect